£3-50
2.99

G000127605

George Gordon, Lord Byron

1788–1824

JARROLD ENGLISH POETS SERIES

Other anthologies include:

Robert and Elizabeth Browning
Samuel Taylor Coleridge
John Keats
Percy Bysshe Shelley
William Wordsworth

LORD BYRON — AN ANTHOLOGY

Designed and produced by Parke Sutton Limited,
8 Thorpe Road, Norwich NR1 1RY for
Jarrold Colour Publications, Barrack Street, Norwich NR3 1TR

This selection first published by Jarrold Colour Publications, 1989

ISBN 0 7117 0440 6

CONTENTS

This series is respectfully dedicated to
St. John Bosco
(1815–1888)
and
Joanna

TO ROMANCE

Parent of golden dreams, Romance!
    Auspicious queen of childish joys,
Who leads't along, in airy dance,
    Thy votive train of girls and boys;
At length, in spells no longer bound,
    I break the fetters of my youth;
No more I tread thy mystic round,
    But leave thy realms for those of Truth.

And yet 'tis hard to quit the dreams
    Which haunt the unsuspicious soul,
Where every nymph a goddess seems,
    Whose eyes through rays immortal roll;
While Fancy holds her boundless reign,
    And all assume a varied hue;
When virgins seem no longer vain,
    And even woman's smiles are true.

And must we own thee but a name,
    And from thy hall of clouds descend?
Nor find a sylph in every dame,
    A Pylades in every friend?

But leave at once thy realms of air
    To mingling bands of fairy elves;
Confess that woman's false as fair,
    And friends have feeling for — themselves!

With shame I own I've felt thy sway;
    Repentant, now thy reign is o'er,
No more thy precepts I obey,
    No more on fancied pinions soar.
Fond fool! to love a sparkling eye,
    And think that eye to truth was dear;
To trust a passing wanton's sigh,
    And melt beneath a wanton's tear!

Romance! disgusted with deceit,
    Far from the motley court I fly,
Where Affectation holds her seat,
    And sickly Sensibility;
Whose silly tears can never flow
    For any pangs excepting thine;
Who turns aside from real woe,
    To steep in dew thy gaudy shrine.

Now join with sable Sympathy,
    With cypress cron'd, array'd in weeds,
Who heaves with thee her simple sigh,
    Whose breast for every bosom bleeds;
And call thy sylvan female choir,
    To mourn a swain for ever gone,
Who once could glow with equal fire,
    But bends not now before thy throne.

Ye genial nymphs, whose ready tears
    On all occasions swiftly flow;
Whose bosoms heave with fancied fears,
    With fancied flames and phrensy glow;
Say, will you mourn my absent name,
    Apostate from your gentle train?
An infant bard at least may claim
    From you a sympathetic strain.

Adieu, fond race! a long adieu!
    The hour of fate is hovering nigh,
E'en now the gulf appears in view,
    Where unlamented you must lie;

Oblivion's blackening lake is seen,
    Convulsed by gales you cannot weather;
Where you, and eke your gentle queen,
    Alas! must perish altogether.

Hours of Idleness

SHE WALKS IN BEAUTY

I

She walks in beauty, like the night
  Of cloudless climes and starry skies;
And all that's best of dark and bright
  Meet in her aspect and her eyes:
Thus mellow'd to that tender light
  Which heaven to gaudy day denies.

II

One shade the more, one ray the less,
  Had half impair'd the nameless grace
Which waves in every raven tress,
  Or softly lightens o'er her face;
Where thoughts serenely sweet express
  How pure, how dear that dwelling-place.

III

And on that cheek, and o'er that brow,
  So soft, so calm, yet eloquent,
The smiles that win, the tints that glow,
  But tell of days in goodness spent,
A mind at peace with all below,
  A heart whose love is innocent!

To A Lady

who presented to the author a lock of hair braided with his own,
and appointed a night in December to meet him in the garden

These locks, which fondly thus entwine,
In firmer chains our hearts confine,
Than all th' unmeaning protestations,
Which swell with nonsense love orations.
Our love is fix'd, I think we've proved it;
Nor time, nor place, nor art have moved it;
Then wherefore should we sigh and whine,
With groundless jealousy repine,
With silly whims and fancies frantic,
Merely to make our love romantic?
Why should you weep like Lydia Languish,
And fret with self-created anguish?
Or doom the lover you have chosen,
On winter nights to sigh half frozen;
In leafless shades to sue for pardon,
Only because the scene's a garden?
For gardens seem, by one consent,
Since Shakspear set the precedent,
Since Juliet first declared her passion,
To form the place of assignation.

Oh! would some modern muse inspire,
And seat her by a sea-coal fire;
Or had the bard at Christmas written,
And laid the scene of love in Britain,
He surely, in commiseration,
Had changed the place of declaration.
In Italy I've no objection;
Warm nights are proper for reflection;
But here our climate is so rigid,
That love itself is rather frigid:
Think on our chilly situation,
And curb this rage for imitation;
Then let us meet, as oft we've done,
Beneath the influence of the sun;
Or, if at midnight I must meet you,
Within your mansion let me greet you:
There we can love for hours together,
Much better, in such snowy weather,
Than placed in all th' Arcadian groves
That ever witness'd rural loves;
Then, if my passion fail to please,
Next night I'll be content to freeze;
No more I'll give a loose to laughter
But curse my fate for ever after.

To A Beautiful Quaker

Sweet girl! though only once we met,
That meeting I shall ne'er forget;
And though we ne'er may meet again,
Remembrance will thy form retain.
I would not say, 'I love,' but still
My senses struggle with my will:
In vain, to drive thee from my breast,
My thoughts are more and more represt;
In vain I check the rising sighs,
Another to the last replies:
Perhaps this is not love, but yet
Our meeting I can ne'er forget.

What though we never silence broke,
Our eyes a sweeter language spoke;
The tongue in flattering falsehood deals,
And tells a tale it never feels:
Deceit the guilty lips impart,
And hush the mandates of the heart;
But soul's interpreters, the eyes,
Spurn such restraint, and scorn disguise.
As thus our glances oft conversed,

And all our bosoms felt rehearsed,
No spirit, from within, reproved us,
Say rather, "twas the spirit moved us.'
Though what they utter'd I repress,
Yet I conceive thou'lt partly guess;
For as on thee my memory ponders,
Perchance to me thine also wanders.
This for myself, at least, I'll say,
Thy form appears through night, through day;
Awake, with it my fancy teems;
In sleep, it smiles in fleeting dreams;
The vision charms the hours away,
And bids me curse Aurora's ray
For breaking slumbers of delight
Which make me wish for endless night.
Since, oh! whate'er my future fate,
Shall joy or woe my steps await,
Tempted by love, by storms beset,
Thine image I can ne'er forget.

Alas! again no more we meet,
No more our former looks repeat;
Then let me breathe this parting prayer,
The dictate of my bosom's care:

'May Heaven so guard my lovely quaker,
That anguish never can o'ertake her;
That peace and virtue ne'er forsake her,
But bliss be aye her heart's partaker!
Oh! may the happy mortal, fated
To be, by dearest ties, related,
For her each hour new joys discover,
And lose the husband in the lover!
May that fair bosom never know
What 'tis to feel the restless woe
Which stings the soul, with vain regret,
Of him who never can forget!'

ELEGY ON NEWSTEAD ABBEY

'It is the voice of years that are gone! they roll before
me with all their deeds.' — OSSIAN.

Newstead! fast-falling, once resplendent dome!
  Religion's shrine! repentant Henry's pride!
Of warriors, monks, and dames the cloister'd tomb,
  Whose pensive shades around thy ruins glide,

Hail to thy pile! more honour'd in thy fall
  Than modern mansions in their pillar'd state;
Proudly majestic frowns thy vaulted hall,
  Scowling defiance on the blasts of fate.

No mail-clad serfs, obedient to their lord,
  In grim array the crimson cross demand;
Or gay assemble round the festive board
  Their chief's retainers, an immortal band:

Else might inspiring Fancy's magic eye
  Retrace their progress through the lapse of time,
Marking each ardent youth, ordain'd to die,
  A votive pilgrim in Judea's clime.

But not from thee, dark pile! departs the chief;
  His feudal realm in other regions lay:
In thee the wounded conscience courts relief,
  Retiring from the garish blaze of day.

Yes! in thy gloomy cells and shades profound
  The monk abjured a world he ne'er could view;
Or blood-stain'd guilt repenting solace found,
  Or innocence from stern oppression flew.

A monarch bade thee from that wild arise,
  Where Sherwood's outlaws once were wont to prowl;
And Superstition's crimes, of various dyes,
  Sought shelter in the priest's protecting cowl.

Where now the grass exhales a murky dew,
  The humid pall of life-extinguish'd clay,
In sainted fame the sacred fathers grew,
  Nor raised their pious voices but to pray.

Where now the bats their wavering wings extend
  Soon as the gloaming spreads her waning shade,
The choir did oft their mingling vespers blend,
  Or matin orisons to Mary paid.

Years roll on years; to ages, ages yield;
    Abbots to abbots, in a line, succeed;
Religion's charter their protecting shield,
    Till royal sacrilege their doom decreed.

One holy Henry rear'd the Gothic walls,
    And bade the pious inmates rest in peace;
Another Henry the kind gift recalls,
    And bids devotion's hallow'd echoes cease.

Vain is each threat or supplicating prayer;
    He drives them exiles from their blest abode,
To roam a dreary world in deep despair —
    No friend, no home, no refuge, but their God.

Hark how the hall, resounding to the strain,
    Shakes with the martial music's novel din!
The heralds of a warrior's haughty reign,
    High crested banners wave thy walls within.

Of changing sentinels the distant hum,
    The mirth of feasts, the clang of burnish'd arms,
The braying trumpet and the hoarser drum,
    Unite in concert with increased alarms.

An abbey once, a regal fortress now,
  Encircled by insulting rebel powers,
War's dread machines o'erhang thy threat'ning brow,
  And dart destruction in sulphureous showers.

Ah vain defence! the hostile traitor's siege,
  Though oft repulsed, by guile o'er-comes the brave;
His thronging foes oppress the faithful liege,
  Rebellion's reeking standards o'er him wave.

Not unavenged the raging baron yields;
  The blood of traitors smears the purple plain;
Unconquer'd still, his falchion there he wields,
  And days of glory yet for him remain.

Still in that hour the warrior wish'd to strew
  Self-gather'd laurels on a self-sought grave;
But Charles' protecting genius hither flew,
  The monarch's friend, the monarch's hope, to save.

Trembling, she snatch'd him from th' unequal strife,
  In other fields the torrent to repel;
For nobler combats, here, reserved his life,
  To lead the band where godlike Falkland fell.

From thee, poor pile! to lawless plunder given,
  While dying groans their painful requiem sound,
Far different incense now ascends to heaven,
  Such victims wallow on the gory ground.

There many a pale and ruthless robber's corse,
  Noisome and ghast, defiles thy sacred sod;
O'er mingling man, and horse commix'd with horse,
  Corruption's heap, the savage spoilers trod.

Graves, long with rank and sighing weeds o'erspread,
  Ransack'd, resign perforce their mortal mould:
From ruffian fangs escape not e'en the dead,
  Raked from repose in search of buried gold.

Hush'd is the harp, unstrung the warlike lyre,
  The minstrel's palsied hand reclines in death;
No more he strikes the quivering chords with fire,
  Or sings the glories of the martial wreath.

At length the sated murderers, gorged with prey,
  Retire: the clamour of the fight is o'er;
Silence again resumes her awful sway,
  And sable Horror guards the massy door.

Here Desolation holds her dreary court:
    What satellites declare her dismal reign!
Shrieking their dirge, ill-omen'd birds resort,
    To flit their vigils in the hoary fane.

Soon a new morn's restoring beams dispel
    The clouds of anarchy from Britain's skies;
The fierce usurper seeks his native hell,
    And Nature triumphs as the tyrant dies.

With storms she welcomes his expiring groans;
    Whirlwinds, responsive, greet his labouring breath;
Earth shudders as her caves receive his bones,
    Loathing the offering of so dark a death.

The legal ruler now resumes the helm,
    He guides through gentle seas the prow of state;
Hope cheers, with wonted smiles, the peaceful realm,
    And heals the bleeding wounds of wearied hate.

The gloomy tenants, Newstead! of thy cells,
    Howling, resign their violated nest;
Again the master on his tenure dwells,
    Enjoy'd, from absence, with enraptured zest.

Vassals, within thy hospitable pale,
Loudly carousing, bless their lord's return;
Culture again adorns the gladdening vale,
And matrons, once lamenting, cease to mourn.

A thousand songs on tuneful echo float,
Unwonted foliage mantles o'er the trees;
And hark! the horns proclaim a mellow note,
The hunters' cry hangs lengthening on the breeze.

Beneath their coursers' hoofs the valleys shake:
What fears, what anxious hopes, attend the chase!
The dying stag seeks refuge in the lake;
Exulting shouts announce the finish'd race.

Ah happy days! too happy to endure!
Such simple sports our plain forefathers knew:
No splendid vices glitter'd to allure;
Their joys were many, as their cares were few.

From these descending, sons to sires succeed;
Time steals along, and Death uprears his dart;
Another chief impels the foaming steed,
Another crowd pursue the panting hart.

Newstead! what saddening change of scene is thine!
    Thy yawning arch betokens slow decay;
The last and youngest of a noble line
    Now holds thy mouldering turrets in his sway.

Deserted now, he scans thy gray worn towers;
    Thy vaults, where dead of feudal ages sleep;
Thy cloisters, pervious to the wintry showers;
    These, these he views, and views them but to weep.

Yet are his tears no emblem of regret:
    Cherish'd affection only bids them flow.
Pride, hope, and love forbid him to forget,
    But warm his bosom with impassion'd glow.

Yet he prefers thee to the gilded domes
    Or gewgaw grottos of the vainly great,
Yet lingers 'mid thy damp and mossy tombs,
    Nor breathes a murmur 'gainst the will of fate.

Haply thy sun, emerging, yet may shine,
    Thee to irradiate with meridian ray;
Hours splendid as the past may still be thine,
    And bless thy future as thy former day.

IF SOMETIMES IN THE HAUNTS OF MEN

If sometimes in the haunts of men
  Thin image from my breast may fade,
The lonely hour presents again
  The semblance of thy gentle shade:
And now that sad and silent hour
  Thus much of thee can still restore,
And sorrow unobserved may pour
  The plaint she dare not speak before.

Oh, pardon that in crowds awhile
  I waste one thought I owe to thee,
And self-condemn'd, appear to smile,
  Unfaithful to thy memory:
Nor deem that memory less dear,
  That then I seem not to repine;
I would not fools should overhear
  One sigh that should be wholly thine.

If not the goblet pass unquaff'd,
  It is not drain'd to banish care;
The cup must hold deadlier draught,
  That brings a Lethe for despair.

And could Oblivion set my soul
    From all her troubled visions free,
I'd dash to earth the sweetest bowl
    That drown'd a single thought of thee.

For wert thou vanish'd from my mind,
    Where could my vacant bosom turn?
And who would then remain behind
    To honour thine abandon'd Urn?
No, no — it is my sorrow's pride
    That last dear duty to fulfil:
Though all the world forget beside,
    'Tis meet that I remember still.

For well I know, that such had been
    The gentle care for him, who now
Unmourn'd shall quit this mortal scene,
    Where none regarded him, but thou:
And, oh! I feel in that was given
    A blessing never meant for me;
Thou wert too like a dream of heaven
    For earthly Love to merit thee.

March 14, 1812.

FARE THEE WELL

'Alas! they had been friends in youth;
But whispering tongues can poison truth;
And constancy lives in realms above;
And life is thorny; and youth is vain;
And to be wroth with one we love,
Doth work like madness in the brain;

But never either found another
To free the hollow heart from paining —
They stood aloof, the scars remaining,
Like cliffs which had been rent asunder;
A dreary sea now flows between,
But neither heat, not frost, nor thunder,
Shall wholly do away, I ween,
The marks of that which once hath been.'
                Coleridge's Christabel.

Fare thee well! and if for ever,
    Still for ever, fare thee well:
Even though unforgiving, never
    'Gainst thee shall my heart rebel.

Would that breast were barred before thee
    Where thy head so oft hath lain.
While that placid sleep came o'er thee
    Which thou ne'er canst know again:

Would that breast, by thee glanced over,
    Every inmost thought could show!
Then thou wouldst at last discover
    'Twas not well to spurn it so.

Though the world for this commend thee —
    Though it smile upon the blow,
Even its praises must offend thee,
    Founded on another's woe:

Though my many faults defaced me,
    Could no other arm be found,
Than the one which once embraced me,
    To inflict a cureless wound?

Yet, oh yet, thyself deceive not;
    Love may sink by slow decay,
But by sudden wrench, believe not
    Hearts can thus be torn away:

Still thine own its life retaineth,
    Still must mine, though bleeding, beat;
And the undying thought which paineth
    Is — that we no more may meet.

These are words of deeper sorrow
    Than the wail above the dead;
Both shall live, but every morrow
    Wake up from a widow'd bed.

And when thou wouldst solace gather,
    When our child's first accents flow,
Wilt thou teach her to say 'Father!'
    Though his care she must forego?

When her little hands shall press thee,
    When her lip to thine is press'd
Think of him whose prayer shall bless thee,
    Think of him thy love had bless'd!

Should her lineaments resemble
    Those thou never more may'st see,
Then thy heart will softly tremble
    With a pulse yet true to me,

All my faults perchance thou knowest,
    All my madness none can know;
All my hopes, where'er thou goest,
    Wither, yet with thee they go.

Every feeling hath been shaken;
    Pride, which not a world could bow,
Bows to thee — by thee forsaken,
    Even my soul forsakes me now:

But 'tis done — all words are idle —
    Words from me are vainer still;
But the thoughts we cannot bridle
    Force their way without the will.

Fare thee well! thus disunited,
    Torn from every nearer tie,
Sear'd in heart, and lone, and blighted,
    More than this I scarce can die.
                    March 17, 1816.

Stanzas to Augusta

I

When all around grew drear and dark,
  And reason half withheld her ray —
And hope but shed a dying spark
  Which more misled my lonely way;

II

In that deep midnight of the mind,
  And that internal strife of heart,
When dreading to be deem'd too kind,
  The weak despair — the cold depart;

III

When fortune changed — and love fled far,
  And hatred's shafts flew thick and fast,
Thou wert the solitary star
  Which rose and set not to the last.

IV

Oh! blest be thine unbroken light!
  That watch'd me as a seraph's eye,
And stood between me the night,
  For ever shining sweetly nigh.

V

And when the cloud upon us came,
  Which strove to blacken o'er thy ray —
Then purer spread its gentle flame,
  And dash'd the darkness all away.

VI

Still may thy spirit dwell on mine,
  And teach it what to brave or brook —
There's more in one soft word of thine
  Than in the world's defied rebuke.

VII

Thou stood'st, as stands a lovely tree,
  That still unbroke, though gently bent,
Still waves with fond fidelity
  Its boughs above a monument.

VIII

The winds might rend — the skies might pour,
  But there thou wert — and still wouldst be
Devoted in the stormiest hour
  To shed thy weeping leaves o'er me.

IX

But thou and thine shall know no blight,
    Whatever fate on me may fall;
For heaven in sunshine will requite
    The kind — and thee the most of all.

X

Then let the ties of baffled love
    Be broken — thine will never break;
Thy heart can feel — but will not move;
    Thy soul, though soft, will never shake.

XI

And these, when all was lost beside,
    Were found and still are fix'd in thee; —
And bearing still a breast so tried,
    Earth is no desert — ev'n to me.

STANZAS TO AUGUSTA

I

Though the day of my destiny's over,
  And the star of my fate hath declined,
Thy soft heart refused to discover
  The faults which so many could find;
Though thy soul with my grief was acquainted,
  It shrunk not to share it with me,
And the love which my spirit hath painted
  It never hath found but in thee.

II

Then when nature around me is smiling,
  The last smile which answers to mine,
I do not believe it beguiling,
  Because it reminds me of thine;
And when winds are at war with the ocean,
  As the breasts I believed in with me,
If their billows excite an emotion,
  It is that they bear me from thee.

III

Though the rock of my last hope is shiver'd,
  And its fragments are sunk in the wave,

Though I feel that my soul is deliver'd
    To pain — it shall not be its slave.
There is many a pang to pursue me:
    They may crush, but they shall not contemn;
They may torture, but shall not subdue me;
    'Tis of thee that I think — not of them.

IV

Though human, thou didst not deceive me,
    Though woman, thou didst not forsake,
Though loved, thou forborest to grieve me,
    Though slander'd, thou never couldst shake;
Though trusted, thou didst not disclaim me,
    Though parted, it was not to fly,
Though watchful, 'twas not to defame me,
    Nor, mute, that the world might belie.

V

Yet I blame not the world, nor despise it,
    Nor the war of the many with one;
If my soul was not fitted to prize it,
    'Twas folly not sooner to shun:
And if dearly that error hath cost me,
    And more than I once could foresee,

I have found that, whatever it lost me,
  It could not deprive me of thee.

VI

From the wreck of the past, which hath perish'd,
  Thus much I at least may recall,
It hath taught me that what I most cherish'd
  Deserved to be dearest of all:
In the desert a fountain is springing,
  In the wide waste there still is a tree,
And a bird in the solitude singing,
  Which speaks to my spirit of thee.

July 24, 1816

To Ianthe

Not in those climes where I have late been straying,
Though Beauty long hath there been matchless deem'd;
Not in those visions to the heart displaying
Forms which it sighs but to have only dream'd,
Hath aught like thee in truth or fancy seem'd:
Nor, having seen thee, shall I vainly seek
To paint those charms which varied as they beam'd —
To such as see thee not my words were weak;
To those who gaze on thee what language could they speak?

Ah! may'st thou ever be what now thou art,
Nor unbeseem the promise of thy spring,
As fair in form, as warm yet pure in heart,
Love's image upon earth without his wing,
And guileless beyond Hope's imagining!
And surely she who now so fondly rears
Thy youth, in thee, thus hourly brightening,
Beholds the rainbow of her future years,
Before whose heavenly hues all sorrow disappears.

Young Peri of the West! — 'tis well for me
My years already doubly number thine;

35

My loveless eye unmoved may gaze on thee,
And safely view thy ripening beauties shine;
Happy, I ne'er shall see them in decline;
Happier, that while all younger hearts shall bleed,
Mine shall escape the doom thine eyes assign
To those whose admiration shall succeed,
But mix'd with pangs to Love's even loveliest hours decreed.

Oh! let that eye, which, wild as the Gazelle's,
Now brightly bold or beautifully shy,
Wins as it wanders, dazzles where it dwells,
Glance o'er this page, nor to my verse deny
That smile for which my breast migh vainly sigh
Could I to thee be ever more than friend:
This much, dear maid, accord; nor question why
To one so young my strain I would commend,
But bid me with my wreath one matchless lily blend.

Such is thy name with this my verse entwined;
And long as kinder eyes a look shall cast
On Harold's page, Ianthe's here enshrined
Shall thus be first beheld, forgotten last:
My days once number'd, should this homage past
Attract thy fairy fingers near the lyre

Of him who hail'd thee lovliest, as thou wast,
   Such is the most my memory may desire;
Though more than Hope can claim, could Friendship less
                                        require?

Childe Harold's Pilgrimage
Canto The First

I

Oh, thou! in Hellas deem'd of heavenly birth,
Muse! form'd or fabled at the minstrel's will!
Since shamed full oft by later lyres on earth,
Mine dares not call thee from thy sacred hill:
Yet there I've wander'd by thy vaunted rill;
Yes! sigh'd o'er Delphi's long deserted shrine,
Where, save that feeble fountain, all is still;
Nor mote my shell awake the weary Nine
To grace so plain a tale — this lowly lay of mine.

II

Whilome in Albion's isle there dwelt a youth,
Who ne in virtue's ways did take delight;
But spent his days in riot most uncouth,
And vex'd with mirth the drowsy ear of Night.
Ah me! in sooth he was a shameless wight,
Sore given to revel and ungodly glee;
Few earthly things found favour in his sight
Save concubines and carnal companie,
And flaunting wassailers of high and low degree.

Childe Harold was he hight: — but whence his name
And lineage long, it suits me not to say;
Suffice it, that perchance they were of fame,
And had been glorious in another day:
But one sad losel soils a name for aye,
However mighty in the olden time;
Nor all that heralds rake from coffin'd clay,
Nor florid prose, nor honeyed lies of rhyme,
Can blazon evil deeds, or consecrate a crime.

IV

Childe Harold bask'd him in the noontide sun,
Disporting there like any other fly;
Nor deem'd before his little day was done
One blast might chill him into misery
But long ere scarce a third of his pass'd by,
Worse than adversity the Childe befell;
He felt the fulness of satiety:
Then loathed he in his native land to dwell,
Which seem'd to him more lone than Eremite's sad cell.

V

For he through Sin's long labyrinth had run,
Nor made atonement when he did amiss,

Had sigh'd to many though he loved but one,
And that loved one, alas! could ne'er be his.
Ah, happy she! to 'scape from him whose kiss
Had been pollution unto aught so chaste;
Who soon had left her charms for vulgar bliss,
And spoil'd her goodly lands to gild his waste,
Nor calm domestic peace had ever deign'd to taste.

VI

And now Childe Harold was sore sick at heart,
And from his fellow bacchanals would flee;
'Tis said, at times the sullen tear would start,
But Pride congeal'd the drop within his ee:
Apart he stalk'd in joyless reverie,
And from his native land resolved to go,
And visit scorching climes beyond the sea;'
With pleasure drugg'd, he almost long'd for woe,
And e'en for change of scene would seek the shades below.

VII

The Childe departed from his father's hall:
It was a vast and venerable pile;
So old, it seemed only not to fall,
Yet strength was pillar'd in easy massy aisle.

Monastic dome! condemn'd to uses vile!
Where Superstition once had made her den
Now Paphian girls were known to sing and smile;
And monks might deem their time was come agen,
If ancient tales say true, nor wrong these holy men.

VIII

Yet oft-times in his maddest mirthful mood
Strange pangs would flash along Childe Harold's brow
As if the memory of some deadly feud
Or disappointed passion lurk'd below:
But this none knew, nor haply cared to know;
For his was not that open, artless soul
That feels relief by bidding sorrow flow,
Nor sought he friend to counsel or condole,
Whate'er this grief mote be, which he could not control.

IX

And none did love him: though to hall and bower
He gather'd revellers from far and near,
He knew them flatt'rers of the festal hour;
The heartless parasites of present cheer.
Yea none did love him — not his lemans dear —
But pomp and power alone are woman's care,

And where these are light Eros finds a feere;
Maidens, like moths, are ever caught by glare,
And Mammon wins his way where Seraphs might despair.

X

Childe Harold had a mother — not forgot,
Though parting from that mother he did shun;
A sister whom he loved, but saw her not
Before his weary pilgrimage begun:
If friends he had, he bade adieu to none.
Yet deem not thence his breast a breast of steel:
Ye, who have known what 'tis to dote upon
A few dear objects, will in sadness feel
Such partings break the heart they fondly hope to heal.

XI

His house, his home, his heritage, his lands,
The laughing dames in whom he did delight,
Whose large blue eyes, fair locks, and snowy hands,
Might shake the saintship of an anchorite,
And long had fed his youthful appetite;
His goblets brimm'd with every costly wine,
And all that mote to luxury invite,
Without a sigh he left, to cross the brine,
And traverse Paynim shores, and pass Earth's central line.

XII

The sails were fill'd, and fair the light winds blew,
As glad to waft him from his native home;
And fast the white rocks faded from his view,
And soon were lost in circumambient foam:
And then, it may be, of his wish to roam
Repented he, but in his bosom slept
The silent thought, nor from his lips did come
One word of wail, whilst others sate and wept,
And to the reckless gales unmanly moaning kept.

XIII

But when the sun was sinking in the sea
He seized his harp, which he at times could string,
And strike albeit with untaught melody,
When deem'd he no strange ear was listening:
And now his fingers o'er it he did fling,
And tuned his farewell in the dim twilight.
While flew the vessel on her snowy wing,
And fleeting shores receded from his sight,
Thus to the elements he pour'd his last 'Good Night.'

I

Adieu, adieu! my native shore
    Fades o'er the waters blue;

The night-winds sigh, the breakers roar,
    And shrieks the wild sea-mew.
Yon sun that sets upon the sea
    We follow in his flight;
Farewell awhile to him and thee,
    My native Land — Good Night!

2

A few short hours and he will rise
    To give the morrow birth;
And I shall hail the main and skies,
    But not my mother earth.
Deserted is my own good hall,
    Its hearth is desolate;
Wild weeds are gathering on the wall;
    My dog howls at the gate.

3

'Come hither, hither, my little page!
    Why dost thou weep and wail?
Or dost thou dread the billows' rage,
    Or tremble at the gale?

But dash the tear-drop from thine eye;
    Our ship is swift and strong:
Our fleetest falcon scarce can fly
    More merrily along.'

4

'Let winds be shrill, let waves roll high,
    I fear not wave nor wind:
Yet marvel not, Sir Childe, that I
    Am sorrowful in mind;
For I have from my father gone,
    A mother whom I love,
And have no friend, save these alone,
    But thee — and one above.

5

'My father bless'd me fervently,
    Yet did not much complain;
But sorely will my mother sigh
    Till I come back again.' —
'Enough, enough, my little lad!
    Such tears become thine eye;
If I thy guileless bosom had,
    Mine own would not be dry.

45

6

'Come hither, hither, my staunch yeoman,
    Why dost thou look so pale?
Or dost thou dread a French foeman?
    Or shiver at the gale?' —
'Deem'st thou I tremble for my life?
    Sir Childe, I'm not so weak;
But thinking on an absent wife
    Will blanch a faithful cheek.

7

'My spouse and boys dwell near thy hall,
    Along the bordering lake,
And when they on their father call,
    What answer shall she make?' —
'Enough, enough, my yeoman good,
    Thy grief let none gainsay;
But I, who am of lighter mood,
    Will laugh to flee away.'

8

For who would trust the seeming sighs
    Of wife or paramour?
Fresh feeres will dry the bright blue eyes
    We late saw streaming o'er.

For pleasures past I do not grieve,
 Nor perils gathering near;
My greatest grief is that I leave
 No thing that claims a tear.

9

And now I'm in the world alone,
 Upon the wide, wide sea:
But why should I for others groan,
 When none will sigh for me?
Perchance my dog will whine in vain,
 Till fed by stranger hands;
But long ere I come back again
 He'd tear me where he stands.

10

With thee, my bark, I'll swifly go
 Athwart the foaming brine;
Nor care what land thou bear'st me to,
 So not again to mine.
Welcome, welcome, ye dark-blue waves!
 And when you fail my sight,
Welcome, ye deserts and ye caves!
 My native Land — Good Night!

XIV

On, on the vessel flies, the land is gone,
And winds are rude in Biscay's sleepless bay.
Four days are sped, but with the fifth, anon,
New shores descried make every bosom gay;
And Cintra's mountain greets them on their way,
And Tagus dashing onward to the deep,
His fabled golden tribute bent to pay;
And soon on board the Lusian pilots leap,
And steer 'twixt fertile shores where yet few rustics reap.

XV

Oh, Christ! it is a goodly sight to see
What Heaven hath done for this delicious land:
What fruits of fragrance blush on every tree!
What goodly prospects o'er the hills expand!
But man would mar them with an impious hand:
And when the Almighty lifts his fiercest scourge
'Gainst those who most transgress his high command,
With treble vengeance will his hot shafts urge
Gaul's locust host, and earth from fellest foemen purge.

XVI

What beauties doth Lisboa first unfold!
Her image floating on that noble tide,

Which poets vainly pave with sands of gold,
But now whereon a thousand keels did ride
Of mighty strength, since Albion was allied,
And to the Lusians did her aid afford:
A nation swoln with ignorance and pride,
Who lick yet loathe the hand that waves the sword
To save them from the wrath of Gaul's unsparing lord.

XVII

But whoso entereth within this town,
That, sheening far, celestial seems to be,
Disconsolate will wander up and down,
'Mid many things unsightly to strange ee;
For hut and palace show like filthily:
The dingy denizens are rear'd in dirt;
Ne personage of high or mean degree
Doth care for cleanness of surtout or shirt;
Though shent with Egypt's plague, unkempt, unwash'd,
                                                    unhurt.

XVIII

Poor, paltry slaves! yet born 'midst noblest scenes —
Why, Nature, waste thy wonders on such men?
Lo! Cintra's glorious Eden intervenes
In variegated maze of mount and glen.

Ah me! what hand can pencil guide, or pen,
To follow half on which the eye dilates
Through views more dazzling unto mortal ken
Than those whereof such things the bard relates,
Who to the awe-struck world unlock'd Elysium's gates?

XIX

The horrid crags, by toppling convent crown'd,
The cork-trees hoar that clothe the shaggy steep,
The mountain-moss by scorching skies imbrown'd,
The sunken glen, whose sunless shrubs must weep,
The tender azure of the unruffled deep,
The orange tints that gild the greenest bough,
The torrents that from cliff to valley leap,
The vine on high, the willow branch below,
Mix'd in one mighty scene, with varied beauty glow.

XX

Then slowly climb the many-winding way,
And frequent turn to linger as you go,
From loftier rocks new loveliness survey,
And rest ye at 'Our Lady's house of woe;'
Where frugal monks their little relics show,
And sundry legends to the stranger tell:

Here impious men have punish'd been, and lo!
Deep in yon cave Honorius long did dwell,
In hope to merit Heaven by making earth a Hell.

XXI

And here and there, as up the crags you spring,
Mark many rude-carved crosses near the path:
Yet deem not these devotion's offering —
These are memorials frail of murderous wrath:
For wheresoe'er the shrieking victim hath
Pour'd forth his blood beneath the assassin's knife,
Some hand erects a cross of mouldering lath;
And grove and glen with thousand such are rife
Throughout this purple land, where law secures not life.

XXII

On sloping mounds, or in the vale beneath,
Are domes where whilome kings did make repair;
But now the wild flowers round them only breathe;
Yet ruin'd splendour still is lingering there,
And yonder towers the Prince's palace fair:
There thou too, Vathek! England's wealthiest son,
Once form'd thy Paradise, as not aware
When wanton Wealth her mightiest deeds hath done,
Meek Peace voluptuous lures was ever wont to shun.

XXIII

Here didst thou dwell, here schemes of pleasure plan,
Beneath yon mountain's ever beauteous brow:
But now, as if a thing unblest by Man,
Thy fairy dwelling is as lone as thou!
Here giant weeds a passage scarce allow
To halls deserted, portals gaping wide:
Fresh lessons to the thinking bosom, how
Vain are the pleasaunces on earth supplied;
Swept into wrecks anon by Time's ungentle tide!

XXIV

Behold the hall where chiefs were late convened!
Oh! dome displeasing unto British eye!
With diadem hight foolscap, lo! a fiend,
A little fiend that scoffs incessantly,
There sits in parchment robe array'd, and by
His side is hung a seal and sable scroll,
Where blazon'd glare names known to chivalry,
And sundry signatures adorn the roll,
Whereat the Urchin points and laughs with all his soul.

XXV

Convention is the dwarfish demon styled
That foil'd the knights in Marialva's dome:

Of brains (if brains they had) he them beguiled,
And turned a nation's shallow joy to gloom.
Here Folly dash'd to earth the victor's plume,
And Policy regain'd what arms had lost:
For chiefs like ours in vain may laurels bloom!
Woe to the conqu'ring, not the conquer'd host,
Since baffled Triumph droops on Lusitania's coast!

XXVI

And ever since that martial synod met,
Britannia sickens, Cintra! at thy name;
And folks in office at the mention fret,
And fain would blush, if blush they could, for shame.
How will posterity the deed proclaim!
Will not our own and fellow nations sneer,
To view these champions cheated of their fame,
By foes in fight o'erthrown, yet victors here,
Where Scorn her finger points through many a coming
year?

XXVII

So deem'd the Childe, as o'er the mountains he
Did take his way in solitary guise:
Sweet was the scene, yet soon he thought to flee,
More restless than the swallow in the skies:

53

Though here awhile he learn'd to moralize,
For Meditation fix'd at times on him;
And conscious Reason whisper'd to depise
His early youth, misspent in maddest whim;
But as he gazed on truth his aching eyes grew dim.

XXVIII

To horse! to horse! he quits, for ever quits
A scene of peace, though soothing to his soul:
Again he rouses from his moping fits,
But seeks not now the harlot and the bowl.
Onward he flies, nor fix'd as yet the goal
Where he shall rest him on his pilgrimage;
And o'er him many changing scenes must roll
Ere toil his thirst for travel can assuage,
Or he shall calm his breast, or learn experience sage.

XXIX

Yet Mafra shall one moment claim delay,
Where dwelt of yore the Lusians' luckless queen;
And church and court did mingle their array,
And mass and revel were alternate seen;
Lordlings and freres — ill-sorted fry I ween!
But here the Babylonian whore hath built

A dome, where flaunts she in such glorious sheen,
  That men forget the blood which she hath spilt,
And bow the knee to Pomp that loves to varnish guilt.

XXX

O'er vales that teem with fruits, romantic hills,
  (Oh, that such hills upheld a free-born race!)
Whereon to gaze the eye with joyaunce fills,
  Childe Harold wends through many a pleasant place.
Though sluggards deem it but a foolish chase,
  An marvel men should quit their easy chair,
The toilsome way, and long, long league to trace,
  Oh! there is sweetness in the mountain air,
And life, that bloated Ease can never hope to share.

XXXI

More bleak to view the hills at length recede,
  And, less luxuriant, smoother vales extend;
Immense horizon-bounded plains succeed!
  Far as the eye discerns, withouten end,
Spain's realms appear whereon her shepherds tend
  Flocks, whose rich fleece right well the trader knows —
Now must the pastor's arm his lambs defend:
  For Spain is compass'd by unyeilding foes,
And all must shield their all, or share Subjection's woes.

Where Lusitania and her Sister meet,
Deem ye what bounds the rival realms divide?
Or ere the jealous queens of nations greet,
Doth Tayo interpose his mighty tide?
Or dark Sierras rise in craggy pride?
Or fence of art, like China's vasty wall? —
Ne barrier wall, ne river deep and wide,
Ne horrid crags, nor mountains dark and tall,
Rise like the rocks that part Hispania's land from Gaul:

XXXIII

But these between a silver streamlet glides,
And scarce a name distinguisheth the brook,
Though rival kingdoms press its verdant sides.
Here leans the idle shepherd on his crook,
And vacant on the rippling waves doth look,
That peacefull still 'twixt bitterest foe-men flow;
For proud each peasant as the noblest duke:
Well doth the Spanish hind the difference know
'Twixt him and Lusian slave, the lowest of the low.

XXXIV

But ere the mingling bounds have far been pass'd,
Dark Guadiana rolls his power along

In sullen billows, murmuring and vast,
So noted ancient roundelays among.
Whilome upon his banks did legions throng
Of Moor and Knight, in mailèd splendour drest:
Here ceased the swift their race, here sunk the strong;
The Paynim turban and the Christian crest
Mix'd on the bleeding stream, by floating hosts oppress'd.

XXXV

Oh, lovely Spain! renown'd, romantic land!
Where is that standard which Pelagio bore,
When Cava's traitor-sire first call'd the band
That dyed thy mountain streams with Gothic gore?
Where are those bloody banners which of yore
Waved o'er thy sons, victorious to the gale,
And drove at last the spoilers to their shore?
Red gleam'd the cross, and waned the crescent pale,
While Afric's echoes thrill'd with Moorish matrons' wail.

XXXVI

Teems not each ditty with the glorious tale?
Ah! such, alas! the hero's amplest fate!
When granite moulders and when records fail,
A peasant's plaint prolongs his dubious date.

Pride! bend thine eyes from heaven to thine estate,
See how the Mighty shrink into a song!
Can Volume, Pillar, Pile preserve thee great?
Or must thou trust Tradition's simple tongue,
When Flattery sleeps with thee, and History does thee
wrong?

XXXVII

Awake, ye sons of Spain! awake! advance!
Lo! Chivalry, your ancient goddess, cries,
But wields not, as of old, her thirsty lance,
Nor shakes her crimson plumage in the skies:
Now on the smoke of blazing bolts she flies,
And speaks in thunder through yon engine's roar:
In every peal she calls — 'Awake! arise!'
Say, is her voice more feeble than of yore,
When her war-song was heard on Andalusia's shore?

XXXVIII

Hark! heard you not those hoofs of dreadful note?
Sounds not the clang of conflict on the heath?
Saw ye not whom the reeking sabre smote,
Nor saved your brethren ere they sank beneath
Tyrants and tyrants' slaves? the fires of death,
The bale-fires on high: — from rock to rock

Each volley tells that thousands cease to breathe;
  Death rides upon the sulphury Siroc,
Red Battle stamps his foot, and nations feel the shock.

XXXIX

Lo! where the Giant on the mountain stands,
  His blood-red tresses deep'ning in the sun,
With death-shot glowing in his fiery hands,
  And eye that scorcheth all it glares upon;
Restless it rolls, now fix'd, and now anon
  Flashing afar, — and at his iron feet
Destruction cowers, to mark what deeds are done;
  For on this morn three potent nations meet,
To shed before his shrine the blood he deems most sweet.

XL

By Heaven! it is a splendid sight to see
  (For one who hath no friend, no brother there)
Their rival scarfs of mix'd embroidery,
  Their various arms that glitter in the air!
What gallant war-hounds rouse them from their lair,
  And gnash their fangs, loud yelling for the prey!
All join the chase, but few the triumph share;
  The Grave shall bear the chiefest prize away,
And Havoc scarce for joy can number their array.

XLI

Three hosts combine to offer sacrifice;
Three tongues prefer strange orisons on high;
Three gaudy standards flout the pale blue skies;
The shouts are France, Spain, Albion, Victory!
The foe, the victim, and the fond ally
That fights for all, but ever fights in vain,
Are met — as if at home they could not die —
To feed the crow on Talavera's plain,
And fertilize the field that each pretends to gain.

XLII

There shall they rot — Ambition's honour'd fools!
Yes, Honour decks the turf that wraps their clay!
Vain Sophistry! in these behold the tools,
The broken tools, that tyrants cast away
By myriads, when they dare to pave their way
With human hearts — to what? — a dream alone.
Can despots compass aught that hails their sway?
Or call with truth one span of earth their own,
Save that wherein at last they crumble bone by bone?

XLIII

Oh, Albuera! glorious field of grief!
As o'er thy plain the Pilgrims prick'd his steed,

Who could foresee thee, in a space so brief,
A scene where mingling foes should boast and bleed!
Peace to the perish'd! may the warrior's meed
And tears of triumph their reward prolong!
Till others fall where other chieftains lead
Thy name shall circle round the gaping throng,
And shine in worthless lays the theme of transient song.

XLIV

Enough of battle's minions! let them play
Their game of lives, and barter breath for fame:
Fame that will scarce reanimate their clay,
Though thousands fall to deck some single name.
In sooth 'twere sad to thwart their noble aim
Who strike, blest hirelings! for their country's good,
And die, that living might have proved her shame;
Perish'd, perchance, in some domestic feud,
Or in a narrower sphere wild Rapine's path pursued.

XLV

Full swiftly Harold wends his lonely way
Where proud Sevilla triumphs unsubdued:
Yet is she free — the spoiler's wish'd-for prey!
Soon, soon shall Conquest's fiery foot intrude,

Blackening her lovely domes with traces rude.
Inevitable hour! 'Gainst fate to strive
Where Desolation plants her famish'd brood
Is vain, or Ilion, Tyre, might yet survive,
And Virtue vanquish all, and murder cease to thrive.

XLVI

But all unconscious of the coming doom,
The feast, the song, the revel here abounds;
Strange modes of merriment the hours consume,
Nor bleed these patriots with their country's wounds;
Nor here War's clarion, but Love's rebeck sounds;
Here Folly still his votaries inthrals;
And young-eyed Lewdness walks her midnight rounds;
Girt with the silent crimes of Capitals,
Still to the last kind Vice clings to the tott'ring walls.

XLVII

Not so the rustic — with his trembling mate
He lurks, nor casts his heavy eye afar,
Lest he should view his vineyard desolate,
Blasted below the dun hot breath of war.
No more beneath soft Eve's consenting star
Fandango twirls his jocund castanet:

Ah, monarchs! could ye taste the mirth ye mar,
  Not in the toils of Glory would ye fret;
The hoarse dull drum would sleep, and Man be happy yet!

XLVIII

How carols now the lusty muleteer?
  Of love, romance, devotion is his lay,
As whilome he was wont the leagues to cheer,
  His quick bells wildly jingling on the way?
No! as he speeds, he chants 'Vivā el Rey!'
  And checks his song to execrate Godoy,
The royal wittol Charles, and curse the day
  When first Spain's queen beheld the black-eyed boy,
And gore-faced Treason sprung from her adulterate joy.

XLIX

On yon long, level plain, at distance crown'd
  With crags, whereon those Moorish turrets rest,
Wide scatter'd hoof-marks dint the wounded ground;
  And, scathed by fire, the greensward's darken'd vest
Tells that the foe was Andalusia's guest:
  Here was the camp, the watch-flame, and the host,
Here the bold peasant storm'd the dragon's nest;
  Still does he mark it with triumphant boast;
And points to yonder cliffs, which oft were won and lost.

And whomsoe'er along the path you meet
Bears in his cap the badge of crimson hue,
Which tells you whom to shun and whom to greet.
Woe to the man that walks in public view
Without of loyalty this token true:
Sharp is the knife, and sudden is the stroke;
And sorely would the Gallic foeman rue,
If subtle poniards, wrapt beneath the cloke,
Could blunt the sabre's edge, or clear the cannon's smoke.

LI

At every turn Morena's dusky height
Sustains aloft the battery's iron load;
And, far as mortal eye can compass sight,
The mountain-howitzer, the broken road,
The bristling palisade, the fosse o'erflow'd,
The station'd bands, the never-vacant watch,
The magazine in rocky durance stow'd,
The holster'd steed beneath the shed of thatch,
The ball-piled pyramid, the ever-blazing match,

LII

Portend the deeds to come: — but he whose nod
Has tumbled feebler despots from their sway,

A moment pauseth ere he lifts the rod;
A little moment deigneth to delay:
Soon will his legions sweep through these their way;
The West must own the Scourger of the world.
Ah! Spain! how sad will be thy reckoning day,
When soars Gaul's Vulture, with his wings unfurl'd,
And thou shalt view thy sons in crowds to Hades hurl'd.

LIII

And must they fall? the young, the proud, the brave,
To swell one bloated Chief's unwholesome reign?
No step between submission and a grave?
The rise of rapine and the fall of Spain?
And doth the Power that man adores ordain
Their doom, nor heed the suppliant's appeal?
Is all that desperate Valour acts in vain?
And Counsel sage, and patriotic Zeal,
The Veteran's skill, Youth's fire, and Manhood's heart of
steel?

LIV

Is it for this the Spanish maid, aroused,
Hangs on the willow her unstrung guitar,
And, all unsex'd, the Anlace hath espoused,
Sung the loud song, and dared the deed of war?

And she, whom once the semblance of a scar
Appall'd, an owlet's 'larum chill'd with dread,
Now views the column-scattering bay'net jar,
The falchion flash, and o'er the yet warm dead
Stalks with Minerva's step where Mars might quake to tread.

LV

Ye who shall marvel when you hear her tale,
Oh! had you known her in her softer hour,
Mark'd her black eye that mocks her coal-black veil,
Heard her light, lively tones in Lady's bower,
Seen her long locks that foil the painter's power,
Her fairy form, with more than female grace,
Scarce would you deem that Saragoza's tower
Beheld her smile in Danger's Gorgon face,
Thin the closed ranks, and lead in Glory's fearful chase.

LVI

Her lover sinks — she sheds no ill-timed tear;
Her chief is slain — she fills his fatal post;
Her fellows flee — she checks their base career;
The foe retires — she heads the sallying host:
Who can appease like her a lover's ghost?
Who can avenge so well a leader's fall?

What maid retrieve when man's flush'd hope is lost?
Who hang so fiercely on the flying Gaul,
Foil'd by a woman's hand, before a batter'd wall?

LVII

Yet are Spain's maids no race of Amazons,
But form'd for all the witching arts of love:
Though thus in arms they emulate her sons,
And in the horrid phalanx dare to move,
'Tis but the tender fierceness of the dove,
Pecking the hand that hovers o'er her mate:
In softness as in firmness far above
Remoter females, famed for sickening prate;
Her mind is nobler sure, her charms perchance as great.

LVIII

The seal Love's dimpling finger hath impress'd
Denotes how soft that chin which bears his touch:
Her lips, whose kisses pout to leave their nest,
Bid man be valiant ere he merit such:
Her glance how wildly beautiful! how much
Hath Phoebus woo'd in vain to spoil her cheek,
Which glows yet smoother from his amorous clutch!
Who round the North for paler dames would seek?
How poor their forms appear! how languid, wan, and weak!

LIX

Match me, ye climes! which poets love to laud;
Match me, ye harems of the land! where now
I strike my strain, far distant, to applaud
Beauties that ev'n a cynic must avow;
Match me those Houries, whom ye scarce allow
To taste the gale lest Love should ride the wind,
With Spain's dark-glancing daughters — deign to know,
There your wise Prophet's paradise we find,
His black-eyed maids of Heaven, angelically kind.

LX

Oh, thou Parnassus! whom I now survey,
Not in the phrensy of a dreamer's eye,
Not in the fabled landscape of a lay,
But soaring snowclad through thy native sky,
In the wild pomp of mountain majesty!
What marvel if I thus essay to sing?
The humblest of thy pilgrims passing by
Would gladly woo thine Echoes with his string,
Though from thy heights no more one Muse will wave her
wing.

LXI

Oft have I dream'd of Thee! whose glorious name
Who knows not, knows not man's divinest lore:

And now I view thee, 'tis, alas! with shame
That I in feeblest accents must adore.
When I recount thy worshippers of yore
I tremble, and can only bend the knee;
Nor raise my voice, nor vainly dare to soar,
But gaze beneath thy cloudy canopy
In silent joy to think at last I look on Thee!

LXII

Happier in this than mightiest bards have been,
Whose fate to distant homes confined their lot,
Shall I unmoved behold the hallow'd scene,
Which others rave of, though they know it not?
Though here no more Apollo haunts his grot,
And thou, the Muses' seat art now their grave,
Some gentle spirit still pervades the spot,
Sighs in the gale, keeps silence in the cave,
And glides with glassy foot o'er yon melodious wave.

LXIII

Of thee hereafter. — Ev'n amidst my strain
I turn'd aside to pay my homage here;
Forgot the land, the sons, the maids of Spain;
Her fate, to every freeborn bosom dear;

And hail'd thee, not perchance without a tear.
Now to my theme — but from thy holy haunt
Let me some remnant, some memorial bear;
Yield me one leaf of Daphne's deathless plant,
Nor let thy votary's hope be deem'd an idle vaunt.

LXIV

But ne'er didst thou, fair Mount, when Greece was

                                              young,

See round thy giant base a brighter choir,
Nor e'er did Delphi, when her priestess sung
The Pythian hymn with more than mortal fire,
Behold a train more fitting to inspire
The song of love, than Andalusia's maids,
Nurst in the glowing lap of soft desire:
Ah! that to these were given such peaceful shades
As Greece can still bestow, though Glory fly her glades.

LXV

Fair is proud Seville; let her country boast
Her strength, her wealth, her site of ancient days;
But Cadiz, rising on the distant coast,
Calls forth a sweeter, though ignoble praise.
Ah, Vice! how soft are thy voluptuous ways!

While boyish blood is mantling, who can 'scape
    The fascination of thy magic gaze?
    A Cherub-hydra round us dost thou gape,
And mould to every taste thy dear delusive shape.

LXVI

When Paphos fell by Time — accursed Time!
    The Queen who conquers all must yield to thee —
    The Pleasures fled, but sought as warm a clime;
    And Venus, constant to her native sea,
    To nought else constant, hither deign'd to flee,
    And fix'd her shrine within these walls of white;
    Though not to one dome circumscribeth she
    Her worship, but, devoted to her rite,
A thousand altars rise, for ever blazing bright.

LXVII

From morn till night, from night till startled Morn
    Peeps blushing on the revel's laughing crew,
    The song is heard, the rosy garland worn;
    Devices quaint, and frolics ever new,
    Tread on each other's kibes. A long adieu
    He bids to sober joy that her sojourns:
    Nought interrupts the riot, though in lieu

Of true devotion monkish incense burns,
And love and prayer unite, or rule the hour by turns.

LXVIII

The Sabbath comes, a day of blessed rest:
What hallows it upon this Christian shore?
Lo! it is sacred to a solemn feast:
Hark! heard you not the forest-monarch's roar?
Crashing the lance, he snuffs the spouting gore
Of man and steed, o'erthrown beneath his horn;
The throng'd arena shakes with shouts for more;
Yells the mad crowd o'er entrails freshly torn,
Nor shrinks the female eye, nor ev'n affects to mourn.

LXIX

The seventh day this; the jubilee of man.
London! right well thou know'st the day of prayer:
Then thy spruce citizen, wash'd artisan,
And smug apprentice gulp their weekly air:
Thy coach of hackney, whiskey, one-horse chair,
And humblest gig through sundry suburbs whirl;
To Hampstead, Brentford, Harrow make repair;
Till the tired jade the wheel forgets to hurl,
Provoking envious gibe from each pedestrian churl.

Some o'er thy Thamis row the ribbon'd fair,
Others along the safer turnpike fly;
Some Richmond-hill ascend, some scud to Ware,
And many to the steep of Highgate hie.
Ask ye, Bœotian shades! the reason why?
'Tis to the worship of the solemn Horn,
Grasp'd in the holy hand of Mystery,
In whose dread name both men and maids are sworn,
And consecrate the oath with draught, and dance till morn.

All have their fooleries — not alike are thine,
Fair Cadiz, rising o'er the dark blue sea!
Soon as the matin bell proclaimeth nine,
Thy Saint-adorers count the rosary:
Much is the Virgin teased to shrive them free
(Well do I ween the only virgin there)
From crimes as numerous as her beadsmen be;
Then to the crowded circus forth they fare:
Young, old, high, low, at once the same diversion share.

The lists are oped, the spacious area clear'd,
Thousands on thousands piled are seated round;

Long ere the first loud trumpet's note is heard,
Ne vacant space for lated wight is found:
Here dons, grandees, but chiefly dames abound,
Skill'd in the ogle of a roguish eye,
Yet ever well inclined to heal the wound;
None through their cold disdain are doom'd to die,
As moon-struck bards complain, by Love's sad archery.

LXXIII

Hush'd is the din of tongues — on gallant steeds,
With milk-white crest, gold spur, and light-poised
lance,
Four cavaliers prepare for venturous deeds,
And lowly bending to the lists advance;
Rich are their scarfs, their chargers featly prance:
If in the dangerous game they shine today,
The crowd's loud shout and ladies' lovely glance,
Best prize of better acts, they bear away,
And all that kings or chiefs e'er gain their toils repay.

LXXIV

In costly sheen and gaudy cloak array'd,
But all afoot, the light-limb'd Matadore
Stands in the centre, eager to invade

The lord of lowing herds; but not before
The ground, with cautious tread, is traversed o'er,
Lest aught unseen should lurk to thwart his speed:
His arms a dart, he fights aloof, nor more
Can man achieve without the friendly steed —
Alas! too oft condemn'd for him to bear and bleed.

LXXV

Thrice sounds the clarions; lo! the signal falls,
The den expands, and Expectation mute
Gapes round the silent circle's peopled walls.
Bounds with one lashing spring the mighty brute,
And, wildly staring, spurns, with sounding foot,
The sand, nor blindly rushes on his foe:
Here, there, he points his threatening front, to suit
His first attack, wide waving to and fro
His angry tail; red rolls his eye's dilated glow.

LXXVI

Sudden he stops; his eye is fix'd: away,
Away, thou heedless boy! prepare the spear:
Now is thy time to perish, or display
The skill that yet may check his mad career.
With well-timed croupe the nimble coursers veer;

On foams the bull, but not unscathed he goes;
Streams from his flank the crimson torrent clear:
He flies, he wheels, distracted with his throes;
Dart follows dart; lance, lance; loud bellowings speak his
woes.

LXXVII

Again he comes; nor dart nor lance avail,
Not the wild plunging of the tortured horse;
Though man and man's avenging arms assail,
Vain are his weapons, vainer is his force.
One gallant steed is stretch'd a mangled corse;
Another, hideous sigh! unseam'd appears,
His gory chest unveils life's panting source;
Though death-struck, still his feeble frame he rears;
Staggering, but stemming all, his lord unharm'd he bears.

LXXVIII

Foil'd, bleeding, breathless, furious to the last,
Full in the centre stands the bull at bay,
Mid wounds, and clinging darts, and lances brast,
And foes disabled in the brutal fray;
And now the Matadores around him play,
Shake the red cloak and poise the ready brand:
Once more through all he bursts his thundering way —

Vain rage! the mantle quits the conynge hand,
Wraps his fierce eye — 'tis past — he sinks upon the sand!

LXXIX

Where his vast neck just mingles with the spine,
Sheathed in his form the deadly weapon lies.
He stops — he starts — disdaining to decline:
Slowly he falls, amidst triumphant cries,
Without a groan, without a struggle dies.
The decorated car appears — on high
The corse is piled — sweet sight for vulgar eyes —
Four steeds that spurn the rein, as swift as shy,
Hurl the dark bulk along, scarce seen in dashing by.

LXXX

Such the ungentle sport that oft invites
The Spanish maid, and cheers the Spanish swain.
Nurtured in blood betimes, his heart delights
In vengeance, gloating on another's pain.
What private feuds the troubled village stain!
Though now one phalanx'd host should meet the foe,
Enough, alas! in humble homes remain,
To mediate 'gainst friends the secret blow,
For some slight cause of wrath whence life's warm stream
must flow.

LXXXI

But Jealousy has fled: his bars, his bolts,
His wither'd centinel, Duenna sage!
And all whereat the generous soul revolts,
Which the stern dotard deem'd he could encage,
Have pass'd to darkness with the vanish'd age.
Who late so free as Spanish girls were seen
(Ere War uprose in his volcanic rage),
With braided tresses bounding o'er the green,
While on the gay dance shone Night's lover-loving Queen?

LXXXII

Oh! many a time and oft, had Harold loved,
Or dream'd he loved, since rapture is a dream;
But now his wayward bosom was unmoved,
For not yet had he drunk of Lethe's stream;
And lately had he learn'd with truth to deem
Love has no gift so grateful as his wings:
How fair, how young, how soft soe'er he seem,
Full from the fount of Joy's delicious springs
Some bitter o'er the flowers its bubbling venom flings.

LXXXIII

Yet to the beauteous form he was not blind,
Though now it moved him as it moves the wise:

78

Not that Philosophy on such a mind
E'er deign'd to bend her chastely-awful eyes:
But Passion raves herself to rest, or flies;
And Vice, that digs her own voluptuous tomb,
Had buried long his hopes, no more to rise:
Pleasure's pall'd victim! life-abhorring gloom
Wrote on his faded brow curst Cain's unresting doom.

LXXXIV

Still he beheld, nor mingled with the throng;
But view'd them not with misanthropic hate:
Fain would he now have join'd the dance, the song;
But who may smile that sinks beneath his fate:
Nought that he saw his sadness could abate:
Yet once he struggled 'gainst the demon's sway,
And as in Beauty's bower he pensive sate,
Pour'd forth his unpremeditated lay,
To charms as fair as those that soothed his happier day.

To Inez

1 *Nay, smile not at my sullen brow;*
   Alas! I cannot smile again:
Yet Heaven avert that ever thou
   Shouldst weep, and haply weep in vain.

2 *And dost thou ask what secret woe*
   I bear, corroding joy and youth?
And wilt thou vainly seek to know
   A pang, ev'n thou must fail to soothe?

3 *It is not love, it is not hate,*
   Nor low Ambition's honours lost,
That bids me loathe my present state,
   And fly from all I prized the most:

4 *It is that weariness which springs*
   From all I meet, or hear, or see:
To me no pleasure Beauty brings;
   Thine eyes have scarce a charm for me.

5   It is that settled, ceaseless gloom
      The fabled Hebrew wanderer bore;
That will not look beyond the tomb,
      But cannot hope for rest before.

6   What Exile from himself can flee?
      To zones though more and more remote,
Still, still pursues, where'er I be,
      The blight of life — the demon Thought.

7   Yet others rapt in pleasure seem,
      And taste of all that I forsake;
Oh! may they still of transport dream,
      And ne'er, at least like me, awake!

8   Through many a clime 'tis mine to go,
      With many a retrospection curst;
And all my solace is to know,
      Whate'er betides, I've known the worst.

9   What is that worst? Nay, do not ask —
      In pity from the search forbear:
Smile on — nor venture to unmask
      Man's heart, and view the Hell that's there.

LXXXV

Adieu, fair Cadiz! yea, a long adieu!
Who may forget how well thy walls have stood?
When all were changing, thou alone wert true,
First to be free, and last to be subdued:
And if amidst a scene, a shock so rude,
Some native blood was seen thy streets to dye
A traitor only fell beneath the feud:
Here all were noble, save Nobility!
None hugg'd a conqueror's chain, save fallen Chivalry!

LXXXVI

Such be the sons of Spain, and strange her fate!
They fight for freedom who were never free,
A Kingless people for a nerveless state;
Her vassals combat when their chieftains flee,
True to the veriest slaves of Treachery:
Fond of a land which gave them nought but life,
Pride points the path that leads to Liberty;
Back to the struggle, baffled in the strife,
War, war is still the cry, 'War even to the knife!'

LXXXVII

Ye, who would more of Spain and Spaniards know,
Go, read whate'er is writ of bloodiest strife:

Whate'er keen Vengeance urged on foreign foe
Can act, is acting there against man's life:
From flashing scimitar to secret knife,
War mouldeth there each weapon to his need —
So may he guard the sister and the wife,
So may he make each curst oppressor bleed —
So may such foes deserve the most remorseless deed!

LXXXVIIII

Flows there a tear of pity for the dead?
Look o'er the ravage of the reeking plain;
Look on the hands with female slaughter red;
Then to the dogs resign the unburied slain,
Then to the vulture let each corse remain,
Albeit unworthy of the prey-bird's maw;
Let their bleach'd bones, and blood's unbleaching stain,
Long mark the battle-field with hideous awe:
Thus only may our sons conceive the scenes we saw!

LXXXIX

Nor yet, alas! the dreadful work is done;
Fresh legions pour adown the Pyrenees:
It deepens still, the work is scarce begun,
Nor mortal eye the distant end foresees.
Fall'n nations gaze on Spain; if freed, she frees

More than her fell Pizarros once enchain'd:
Strange retribution! now Columbia's ease
Repairs the wrongs that Quito's sons sustain'd,
While o'er the parent clime prowls Murder unrestrain'd.

XC

Not all the blood at Talavera shed,
Not all the marvels of Barossa's fight,
Not Albuera lavish of the dead,
Have won for Spain her well-asserted right.
When shall her Olive-Branch be free from blight?
When shall she breathe her from the blushing toil?
How many a doubtful day shall sink in night,
Ere the Frank robber turn him from his spoil,
And Freedom's stranger-tree grow native of the soil!

XCI

And thou, my friend! — since unavailing woe
Bursts from my heart, and mingles with the strain —
Had the sword laid thee with the mighty low,
Pride might forbid e'en Friendship to complain:
But thus unlaurel'd to descend in vain,
By all forgotten, save the lonely breast,
And mix unbleeding with the boasted slain,

While Glory crowns so many a meaner crest!
What hadst thou done to sink so peacefully to rest?

XCII

Oh, known the earliest, and esteem'd the most!
Dear to a heart where nought was left so dear!
Though to my hopeless days for ever lost,
In dreams deny me not to see thee here!
And Morn in secret shall renew the tear
Of Consciousness awaking to her woes,
And Fancy hover o'er thy bloodless bier,
Till my frail frame return to whence it rose,
And mourn'd and mourner lie united in repose.

XCIII

Here is one fytte of Harold's pilgrimage:
Ye who of him may further seek to know,
Shall find some tidings in a future page,
If he that rhymeth now may scribble moe.
Is this too much? stern Critic! say not so:
Patience! and ye shall hear what he beheld
In other lands, where he was doom'd to go:
Lands that contain the monuments of Eld,
Ere Greece and Grecian arts by barbarous hands were
quell'd.

LARA

CANTO THE FIRST

I

The Serfs are glad through Lara's wide domain,
And Slavery half forgets her feudal chain;
He, their unhoped, but unforgotten lord,
The long self-exiled chieftain, is restored:
There be bright faces in the busy hall,
Bowls on the board, and banners on the wall;
Far checkering o'er the pictured window, plays
the unwonted faggot's hospitable blaze;
And gay retainers gather round the hearth,
With tongues all loudness, and with eyes all mirth.

II

The chief of Lara is returned again:
And why had Lara cross'd the bounding main?
Left by his sire, too young such loss to know,
Lord of himself, — that heritage of woe,
That fearful empire which the human breast
But holds to rob the heart within of rest! —
With none to check, and few to point in time
The thousand paths that slope the way to crime;

Then, when he most required commandment, then
Had Lara's daring boyhood govern'd men.
It skills not, boots not step by step to trace
His youth through all the mazes of its race;
Short was the course his restlessness had run,
But long enough to leave him half undone.

III

And Lara left in youth his father-land;
But from the hour he waved his parting hand
Each trace wax'd fainter of his course, till all
Had nearly ceased his memory to recall.
His sire was dust, his vassals could declare,
'Twas all they knew, that Lara was not there;
Nor send, nor came he, till conjecture grew
Cold in the many, anxious in the few.
His hall scarce echoes with his wonted name,
His portrait darkens in its fading frame,
Another chief consoled his destined bride,
The young forgot him, and the old had died;
'Yet doth he live!' exclaims the impatient heir,
And sighs for sables which he must not wear.
A hundred scutcheons deck with gloomy grace
The Laras' last and longest dwelling-place;

But one is absent from the mouldering file,
That now were welcome in that Gothic pile.

IV

He comes at last in sudden loneliness,
And whence they know not, why they need not guess;
They more might marvel, when the greeting's o'er,
Not that he came, but came not long before:
No train is his beyond a single page,
Of foreign aspect, and of tender age.
Years had roll'd on, and fast they speed away
To those that wander as to those that stay;
But lack of tidings from another clime
Had lent a flagging wing to weary Time.
They see, they recognise, yet almost deem
The present dubious, or the past a dream.

He lives, nor yet is past his manhood's prime,
Though sear'd by toil, and something touch'd by time;
His faults, whate'er they were, if scarce forgot,
Might be untaught him by his varied lot;
Nor good nor ill of late were known, his name
Might yet uphold his patrimonial fame:
His soul in youth was haughty, but his sins
No more than pleasure from the stripling wins;

And such, if not yet harden'd in their course,
Might be redeem'd, nor ask a long remorse.

V

And they indeed were changed — 'tis quickly seen,
Whate'er he be, 'twas not what he had been:
That brow in furrow'd lines had fix'd at last,
And spake of passions, but of passion past:
The pride, but not the fire, of early days,
Coldness of mien, and carelessness of praise;
A high demeanour, and a glance that took
Their thoughts from others by a single look;
And that sarcastic levity of tongue,
The stinging of a heart the world hath stung,
That darts in seeming playfulness around,
And makes those feel that will not own the wound;
All these seem'd his, and something more beneath
Than glance could well reveal, or accent breathe.
Ambition, glory, love, the common aim,
That some can conquer, and that all would claim,
Within his breast appear'd no more to strive,
Yet seem'd as lately they had been alive;
And some deep feeling it were vain to trace
At moments lighten'd o'er his livid face.

VI

Not much he loved long question of the past,
Nor told of wondrous wilds, and deserts vast,
In those far lands where he had wander'd lone,
And — as himself would have it seem — unknown;
Yet these in vain his eye could scarcely scan,
Nor glean experience from his fellow man;
But what he had beheld he shunn'd to show,
As hardly worth a stranger's care to know;
If still more prying such inquiry grew,
His brow fell darker, and his words more few.

VII

Not unrejoiced to see him once again,
Warm was his welcome to the haunts of men;
Born of high lineage, link'd in high command,
He mingled with the magnates of his land;
Join'd the carousals of the great and gay,
And saw them smile or sigh their hours away;
But still he only saw, and did not share,
The common pleasure or the general care;
He did not follow what they all pursued
With hope still baffled, still to be renew'd;

Nor shadowy honour, nor substantial gain,
Nor beauty's preference, and the rival's pain:
Around him some mysterious circle thrown
Repell'd approach, and show'd him still alone;
Upon his eye sat something of reproof,
That kept at least frivolity aloof;
And things more timid that beheld him near
In silence gazed, or whisper'd mutual fear;
And they the wiser, friendlier few confess'd
They deem'd him better than his air express'd.

VIII

'Twas strange — in youth all action and all life,
Burning for pleasure, not averse from strife;
Woman, the field, the ocean, all that gave
Promise of gladness, peril of a grave,
In turn he tried — he ransack'd all below,
And found his recompense in joy or woe,
No tame, trite medium; for his feelings sought
In that intenseness an escape from thought:
The tempest of his heart in scorn had gazed
On that the feebler elements had raised;
The rapture of his heart had look'd on high,
And ask'd if greater dwelt beyond the sky:

Chain'd to excess, the slave of each extreme,
How woke he from the wildness of that dream?
Alas! he told not — but he did awake
To curse the wither'd heart that would not break.

IX

Books, for his volume heretofore was Man,
With eye more curious he appear'd to scan,
And oft, in sudden mood, for many a day,
From all communion he would start away:
And then, his rarely call'd attendants said,
Through night's long hours would sound his hurried tread
O'er the dark gallery, where his fathers frown'd
In rude but antique portraiture around:
They heard, but whisper'd — 'that must not be known —
The sound of words less earthly than his own.
Yes, they who chose might smile, but some had seen
They scarce knew what, but more than should have been.
Why gazed he so upon the ghastly head
Which hands profane had gather'd from the dead,
That still beside his open'd volume lay,
As if to startle all save him away?
Why slept he not when others were at rest?
Why heard no music, and received no guest?

All was not well, they deem'd — but where the wrong?
Some knew perchance — but 'twere a tale too long;
And such besides were too discreetly wise,
To more than hint their knowledge in surmise;
But if they would — they could' — around the board
Thus Lara's vassals prattled of their lord.

X

It was the night — and Lara's glassy stream
The stars are studding, each with imaged beam;
So calm, the waters scarcely seem to stray,
And yet they glide like happiness away;
Reflecting far and fairy-like from high
The immortal lights that live along the sky:
Its banks are fringed with many a goodly tree,
And flowers the fairest that may feast the bee;
Such in her chaplet infant Dian wove,
And Innocence would offer to her love.
These deck the shore; the waves their channel make
In windings bright and mazy like the snake.
All was so still, so soft in earth and air,
You scarce would start to meet a spirit there;
Secure that nought of evil could delight
To walk in such a scene, on such a night!

It was a moment only for the good:
So Lara deem'd, nor longer there he stood,
But turn'd in silence to his castle-gate;
'Such scene his soul no more could contemplate:
Such scene reminded him of other days,
Of skies more cloudless, moons of purer blaze,
Of nights more soft and frequent, hearts that now —
No — no — the storm may beat upon his brow,
Unfelt, unsparing — but a night like this,
A night of beauty, mock'd such breast as his.

XI

He turn'd within his solitary hall,
And his high shadow shot along the wall:
There were the painted forms of other times,
'Twas all they left of virtues or of crimes,
Save vague tradition; and the gloomy vaults
That hid their dust, their foibles, and their faults;
And half a column of the pompous page,
That speeds the specious tale from age to age;
Where history's pen its praise or blame supplies,
And lies like truth, and still most truly lies.
He wandering mused, and as the moonbeam shone
Through the dim lattice o'er the floor of stone,

And the high fretted roof, and saints, that there
O'er Gothic windows knelt in pictured prayer,
Reflected in fantastic figures grew,
Like life, but not like mortal life to view:
His bristling locks of sable, brow of gloom,
And the wide waving of his shaken plume,
Glanced like a spectre's attributes, and gave
His aspects all that terror gives the grave.

XII

'Twas midnight — all was slumber; the lone light
Dimm'd in the lamp, as loth to break the night.
Hark! there be murmurs heard in Lara's hall —
A sound, a voice, a shriek, a fearful call!
A long, loud shriek — and silence — did they hear
That frantic echo burst the sleeping ear?
They heard and rose, and, tremulously brave,
Rush where the sound invoked their aid to save;
They come with half-lit tapers in their hands,
And snatch'd in startled haste unbelted brands.

XIII

Cold as the marble where his length was laid,
Pale as the beam that o'er his features play'd,

Was Lara stretch'd; his half-drawn sabre near,
Dropp'd it should seem in more than nature's fear;
Yet he was firm, or had been firm till now,
And still defiance knit his gather'd brow;
Though mix'd with terror, senseless as he lay,
There lived upon his lip the wish to slay;
Some half-form'd threat in utterance there had died,
Some imprecation of despairing pride;
His eye was almost seal'd, but not forsook,
Even in its trance, the gladiator's look,
That oft awake his aspect could disclose,
And now was fix'd in horrible repose.
They raise him — bear him: — hush! he breathes, he speaks,
The swarthy blush recolours in his cheeks,
His lip resumes its red, his eye, though dim,
Rolls wide and wild, each slowly quivering limb
Recalls its function, but his words are strung
In terms that seem not of his native tongue;
Distinct but strange, enough they understand
To deem them accents of another land;
And such they were, and meant to meet an ear
That hears him not — alas! that cannot hear!

XIV

His page approach'd, and he alone appear'd
To know the import of the words they heard;
And, by the changes of his cheek and brow,
They were not such as Lara should avow,
Nor he interpret, — yet with less surprise
Than those around their chieftain' state he eyes,
But Lara's prostrate form he bent beside,
And in that tongue which seem'd his own replied,
And Lara heeds those tones that gently seem
To soothe away the horrors of his dream —
If dream it were that thus could overthrow
A breast that needed not ideal woe.

XV

Whate'er his frenzy dream'd or eye beheld, —
If yet remember'd ne'er to be reveal'd, —
Rests at his heart: the custom'd morning came,
And breathed new vigour in his shaken frame;
And solace sought he none from priest nor leech,
And soon the same in movement and in speech,
As heretofore he fill'd the passing hours,
Nor less he smiles, nor more his forehead lowers,

Than these were wont; and if the coming night
Appear'd less welcome now to Lara's sight,
He to his marvelling vassals show'd it not,
Whose shuddering proved their fear was less forgot.
In trembling pairs (alone they dared not) crawl
The astonish'd slaves, and shun the fated hall;
The waving banner, and the clapping door,
The rustling tapestry, and the echoing floor;
The long dim shadows of surrounding trees,
The flapping bat, the night song of the breeze;
Aught they behold or hear their thought appals,
As evening saddens o'er the dark grey walls.

XVI

Vain thought! that hour of ne'er unravell'd gloom
Came not again, or Lara could assume
A seeming of forgetfulness, that made
His vassals more amazed nor less afraid.
Had memory vanish'd then with sense restored?
Since word, nor look, nor gesture of their lord
Beatray'd a feeling that recall'd to these
That fever'd moment of his mind's disease.
Was it a dream? was his the voice that spoke
Those strange wild accents; his the cry that broke

Their slumber? his the oppress'd, o'er-labour'd heart
That ceased to beat, the look that made them start?
Could he who thus had suffer'd so forget,
When such as saw that suffering shudder yet?
Or did that silence prove his memory fix'd
Too deep for words, indelible, unmix'd
In that corroding secrecy which gnaws
The heart to show the effect, but not the cause?
Not so in him; his breast had buried both,
Nor common gazers could discern the growth
Of thoughts that mortal lips must leave half told;
They choke the feeble words that would unfold.

XVII

In him inexplicably mix'd appear'd
Much to be loved and hated, sought and fear'd;
Opinion varying o'er his hidden lot,
In praise or railing ne'er his name forgot:
His silence form'd a theme for others' prate —
They guess'd, they gazed, they fain would know his fate.
What had he been? what was he, thus unknown,
Who walk'd their world, his lineage only known?
A hater of his kind? yet some would say,
With them he could seem gay amidst the gay;

But own'd that smile, if oft observed and near,
Waned in its mirth, and wither'd to a sneer;
That smile might reach his lip, but pass'd not by,
None e'er could trace its laughter to his eye:
Yet there was softness too in his regard,
At times, a heart as not by nature hard,
But once perceived, his spirit seem'd to chide
Such weakness, as unworthy of its pride,
And steel'd itself, as scorning to redeem
One doubt from others' half-withheld esteem;
In self-inflicted penance of a breast
Which tenderness might once have wrung from rest;
In vigilance of grief that would compel
The soul to hate for having loved too well.

XVIII

There was in him a vital scorn of all:
As if the worst had fall'n which could befall,
He stood a stranger in this breathing world,
An erring spirit from another hurl'd;
A thing of dark imaginings, that shaped
By choice the perils he by chance escaped;
But 'scaped in vain, for in their memory yet
His mind would half exult and half regret:

With more capacity for love than earth
Bestows on most of mortal mould and birth,
His early dreams of good outstripp'd the truth,
And troubled manhood follow'd baffled youth;
With thought of years in phantom chase mis-spent,
And wasted powers for better purpose lent;
And fiery passions that had pour'd their wrath
In hurried desolation o'er his path,
And left the better feelings all at strife
In wild reflection o'er his stormy life;
But haughty still, and loth himself to blame,
He call'd on Nature's self to share the shame,
And charged all faults upon the fleshly form
She gave to clog the soul, and feast the worm;
Till he at last confounded good and ill,
And half mistook for fate the acts of will;
Too high for common selfishness, he could
At times resign his own for others' good,
But not in pity, not because he ought,
But in some strange perversity of thought,
That sway'd him onward with a secret pride
To do what few or none would do beside;
And this same impulse would, in tempting time,
Mislead his spirit equally to crime;

So much he soar'd beyond, or sunk beneath,
The men with whom he felt condemn'd to breathe,
And long'd by good or ill to separate
Himself from all who shared his mortal state;
His mind abhorring this, had fix'd her throne
Far from the world, in regions of her own:
Thus coldly passing all that pass'd below,
His blood in temperate seeming now would flow:
Ah! happier if it ne'er with guilt had glow'd,
But ever in that icy smoothness flow'd!
'Tis true, with other men their path he walk'd,
And like the rest in seeming did and talk'd,
Nor outraged Reason's rules by flaw nor start,
His madness was not of the head, but heart;
And rarely wander'd in his speech, or drew
His thoughts so forth as to offend the view.

XIX

With all that chilling mystery of mien,
And seeming gladness to remain unseen,
He had (if 'twere not nature's boon) an art
Of fixing memory on another's heart:
It was not love perchance, nor hate, nor aught
That words can image to express the thought;

But they who saw him did not see in vain,
And once beheld, would ask of him again:
And those to whom he spake remember'd well,
And on the words, however light, would dwell:
None knew nor how, nor why, but he entwined
Himself perforce around the hearer's mind;
There he was stamp'd, in liking, or in hate,
If greeted once; however brief the date
That friendship, pity, or aversion knew,
Still there within the inmost thought he grew.
You could not penetrate his soul, but found,
Despite your wonder, to your own he wound;
His presence haunted still; and from the breast
He forced an all unwilling interest:
Vain was the struggle in that mental net,
His spirit seem'd to dare you to forget!

XX

There is a festival, where knights and dames,
And aught that wealth or lofty lineage claims,
Appear — a high-born and a welcome guest
To Otho's hall came Lara with the rest.
The long carousal shakes the illumined hall,
Well speeds alike the banquet and the ball;

And the gay dance of bounding Beauty's train
Links grace and harmony in happiest chain:
Blest are the early hearts and gentle hands;
That mingle there in well according bands;
It is a sight the careful brow might smooth,
And make Age smile, and dream itself to youth,
And Youth forget such hour was past on earth,
So springs the exulting bosom to that mirth!

XXI

And Lara gazed on these, sedately glad,
His brow belied him if his soul was sad;
And his glance follow'd fast each fluttering fair,
Whose steps of lightness woke no echo there:
He lean'd against the lofty pillar nigh,
With folded arms and long attentive eye,
Nor mark'd a glance so sternly fix'd on his —
Ill brook'd high Lara scrutiny like this:
At length he caught it, 'tis a face unknown,
But seems as searching his, and his alone;
Prying and dark, a stranger's by his mien,
Who still till now had gazed on him unseen:
At length encountering meets the mutual gaze
Of keen inquiry, and of mute amaze;

On Lara's glance emotion gathering grew,
As if distrusting that the stranger threw;
Along the stranger's aspect, fix'd and stern,
Flash'd more than thence the vulgar eye could learn.

XXII

'Tis he!' the stranger cried, and those that heard
Re-echoed fast and far the whisper'd word.
'Tis he!' — 'Tis who?' they question far and near,
Till louder accents rung on Lara's ear;
So widely spread, few bosoms well could brook
The general marvel, or that single look:
But Lara stirr'd not, changed not, the surprise
That sprung at first to his arrested eyes
Seem'd now subsided, neither sunk nor raised
Glanced his eye round, though still the stranger gazed;
And drawing nigh, exclaim'd, with haughty sneer,
'Tis he! how came he thence? — what doth he here?'

XXIII

It were too much for Lara to pass by
Such questions, so repeated fierce and high;
With look collected, but with accent cold,
More mildly firm than petulantly bold,

He turn'd, and met the inquisitorial tone —
'My name is Lara! — when thine own is known,
Doubt not my fitting answer to requite
The unlook'd-for courtesy of such a knight.
'Tis Lara! — further wouldst thou mark or ask?
I shun no question, and I wear no mask.'

'Thou shunn'st no question! Ponder — is there none
Thy heart must answer, though thine ear would shun?
And deem'st thou me unknown too? Gaze again!
At least thy memory was not given in vain.
Oh! never canst thou cancel half her debt,
Eternity forbids thee to forget.'
With slow and searching glance upon his face
Grew Lara's eyes, but nothing there could trace
They knew, or chose to know — with dubious look
He deign'd no answer, but his head he shook,
And half contemptuous turn'd to pass away;
But the stern stranger motion'd him to stay.

'A word! — I charge thee stay, and answer here
To one, who, wert thou noble, were thy peer,
But as thou wast and art — nay, frown not, lord,
If false, 'tis easy to disprove the word —

But as thou wast and art, on thee looks down,
Distrust thy smiles, but shakes not at thy frown.
Art thou not he? whose deeds ——'

                          'Whate'er I be,
Words wild as these, accusers like to thee,
I list no further; those with whom they weigh
May hear the rest, nor venture to gainsay
The wondrous tale no doubt thy tongue can tell,
Which thus begins so courteously and well.
Let Otho cherish here his polish'd guest,
To him my thanks and thoughts shall be express'd.'
And here their wondering host hath interposed —
'Whate'er there be between you undisclosed,
This is no time nor fitting place to mar
The mirthful meeting with a wordy war.
If thou, Sir Ezzelin, has aught to show
Which it befits Count Lara's ear to know,
To-morrow, here, or elsewhere, as may best
Beseem your mutual judgment, speak the rest;
I pledge myself for thee, as not unknown,
Though, like Count Lara, now return'd alone
From other lands, almost a stranger grown;
And if from Lara's blood and gentle birth
I augur right of courage and of worth,

He will not that untainted line belie,
Nor aught that knighthood may accord, deny.'

'*To-morrow be it,*' Ezzelin replied,
'*And here our several worth and truth be tried;*
I gage my life, my falchion to attest
My words, so may I mingle with the blest!'
What answers Lara? to its centre shrunk
His soul, in deep abstraction sudden sunk;
The words of many, and the eyes of all
That there were gather'd, seem'd on him to fall;
But his were silent, his appear'd to stray
In far forgetfulness away — away —
Alas! that heedlessness of all around
Bespoke remembrance only too profound.

XXIV

'*To-morrow! — ay, to-morrow!'* further word
Than those repeated none from Lara heard:
Upon his brow no outward passion spoke;
From his large eye no flashing anger broke;
Yet there was something fix'd in that low tone,
Which show'd resolve, determined, though unknown.

He seized his cloak — his head he slightly bow'd,
And passing Ezzelin, he left the crowd;
And as he pass'd him, smiling met the frown
With which that chieftain's brow would bear him down:
It was nor smile of mirth, nor struggling pride
That curbs to scorn the wrath it cannot hide:
But that of one in his own heart secure
Of all that he would do, or could endure.
Could this mean peace? the calmness of the good?
Or guilt grown old in desperate hardihood?
Alas! too like in confidence are each,
For man to trust to mortal look or speech;
From deeds, and deeds alone, may he discern
Truths which it wrings the unpractised heart to learn.

XXV

And Lara call'd his page, and went his way —
Well could that stripling word or sign obey:
His only follower from those climes afar,
Where the soul glows beneath a brighter star;
For Lara left the shore from whence he sprung,
In duty patient, and sedate though young;
Silent as him he served, his faith appears
Above his station, and beyond his years.

Though not unknown the tongue of Lara's land,
In such from him he rarely heard command;
But fleet his step, and clear his tones would come,
When Lara's lip breathed forth the words of home:
Those accents, as his native mountains dear,
Awake their absent echoes in his ear,
Friends', kindred's, parents' wonted voice recall,
Now lost, abjured, for one — his friend, his all:
For him earth now disclosed no other guide;
What marvel then he rarely left his side?

XXVI

Light was his form, and darkly delicate
That brow whereon his native sun had sate,
But had not marr'd, though in his beams he grew,
The cheek where oft the unbidden blush shone through;
Yet not such blush as mounts when health would show
All the heart's hue in that delighted glow;
But 'twas a hectic tint of secret care
That for a burning moment fever'd there;
And the wild sparkle of his eye seem'd caught
From high, and lighten'd with electric thought,
Though its black orb those long low lashes' fringe
Had temper'd with a melancholy tinge;

Yet less of sorrow than of pride was there,
Or, if 'twere grief, a grief that none should share:
And pleased not him the sports that please his age,
The tricks of youth, the frolics of the page;
For hours on Lara he would fix his glance,
As all-forgotten in that watchful trance;
And from his chief withdrawn, he wander'd lone,
Brief were his answers, and his questions none;
His walk the wood, his sport some foreign book;
His resting-place the bank that curbs the brook;
He seem'd, like him he served, to live apart
From all that lures the eye, and fills the heart;
To know no brotherhood, and take from earth
No gift beyond that bitter boon — our birth.

XXVII

If aught he loved, 'twas Lara; but was shown
His faith in reverence and in deeds alone;
In mute attention; and his care, which guess'd
Each wish, fulfill'd it ere the tongue express'd.
Still there was haughtiness in all he did,
A spirit deep that brook'd not to be chid;
His zeal, though more than that of servile hands,
In act alone obeys, his air commands;

As if 'twas Lara's less than his desire
That thus he served, but surely not for hire.
Slight were the tasks enjoin'd him by his lord,
To hold the stirrup, or to bear the sword;
To tune his lute, or, if he will'd it more,
On tomes of other times and tongues to pore;
But ne'er to mingle with the menial train,
To whom he show'd nor deference nor disdain,
But that well-worn reserve which proved he knew
No sympathy with that familiar crew:
His soul, whate'er his station or his stem,
Could bow to Lara, not descend to them.
Of higher birth he seem'd, and better days,
Nor mark of vulgar toil that hand betrays,
So femininely white it might bespeak
Another sex, when match'd with that smooth cheek,
But for his garb, and something in his gaze,
More wild and high than woman's eye betrays;
A latent fierceness that far more became
His fiery climate than his tender frame:
True, in his words it broke not from his breast,
But from his aspect might be more than guess'd.
Kaled his name, though rumour said he bore
Another ere he left his mountain-shore:

For sometimes he would hear, however nigh,
That name repeated loud without reply,
As unfamiliar, or, if roused again,
Start to the sound, as but remember'd then;
Unless 'twas Lara's wonted voice that spake,
For then, ear, eyes, and heart would all awake.

XXVIII

He had look'd down upon the festive hall,
And mark'd that sudden strife so mark'd of all:
And when the crowd around and near him told
Their wonder at the calmness of the bold,
Their marvel how the high-born Lara bore
Such insult from a stranger, doubly sore,
The colour of young Kaled went and came,
The lip of ashes, and the cheek of flame;
And o'er his brow the dampening heartdrops threw
The sickening iciness of that cold dew,
That rises as the busy bosom sinks
With heavy thoughts from which reflection shrinks.
Yes — there be things which we must dream and dare,
And execute ere thought be half aware:
Whate'er might Kaled's be, it was enow
To seal his lip, but agonise his brow.

He gazed on Ezzelin till Lara cast
That sidelong smile upon the knight he pass'd;
When Kaled saw that smile his visage fell,
As if on something recognised right well:
His memory read in such a meaning more
Than Lara's aspect unto others wore:
Forward he sprung — a moment, both were gone,
And all within that hall seem'd left alone;
Each had so fix'd his eye on Lara's mien,
All had so mix'd their feelings with that scene,
That when his long dark shadow through the porch
No more relieves the glare of yon high torch,
Each pulse beats quicker, and all bosoms seem
To bound as doubting from too black a dream,
Such as we know is false, yet dread in sooth,
Because the worst is ever nearest truth.
And they are gone — but Ezzelin is there,
With thoughtful visage and imperious air;
But long remain'd not; ere an hour expired
He waved his hand to Otho and retired.

XXIX

The crowd are gone, the revellers at rest;
The courteous host, and all-approving guest,

Again to that accustom'd couch must creep
Where joy subsides, and sorrow sighs to sleep,
And man, o'erlabour'd with his being's strife,
Shrinks to that sweet forgetfulness of life:
There lie love's feverish hope, and cunning's guile,
Hate's working brain, and lull'd ambition's wile;
O'er each vain eye oblivion's pinions wave,
And quench'd existence crouches in a grave.
What better name may slumber's bed become?
Night's sepulchre, the universal home,
Where weakness, strength, vice, virtue, sunk supine,
Alike in naked helplessness recline;
Glad for a while to heave unconscious breath,
Yet wake to wrestle with the dread of death,
And shun, though day but dawn on ills increased,
That sleep, the loveliest, since it dreams the least.

CANTO THE SECOND

I

Night wanes — the vapours round the mountains curl'd
Melt into morn, and Light awakes the world,
Man has another day to swell the past,
And lead him near to little but his last:

But mighty Nature bounds as from her birth,
The sun is in the heavens, and life on earth;
Flowers in the valley, splendour in the beam,
Health on the gale, and freshness in the stream.
Immortal man! behold her glories shine,
And cry, exulting inly, 'They are thine!'
Gaze on, while yet thy gladden'd eye may see:
A morrow comes when they are not for thee:
And grieve what may above thy senseless bier,
Nor earth nor sky will yield a single tear;
Nor cloud shall gather more, nor leaf shall fall,
Nor gale breathe forth one sigh for thee, for all;
But creeping things shall revel in their spoil,
And fit thy clay to fertilise the soil.

II

'Tis morn — 'tis noon — assembled in the hall,
The gather'd chieftains come to Otho's call;
'Tis now the promised hour, that must proclaim
The life or death of Lara's future fame;
And Ezzelin his charge may here unfold,
And whatsoe'er the tale, it must be told.
His faith was pledged, and Lara's promise given,
To meet it in the eye of man and heaven.

Why comes he not? Such truths to be divulged,
Methinks the accuer's rest is long indulged.

III

The hour is past and Lara too is there,
With self-confiding, coldly patient air;
Why comes not Ezzelin? The hour is past,
And murmurs rise, and Otho's brow's o'ercast.
'I know my friend! his faith I cannot fear,
If yet he be on earth, expect him here;
The roof that held him in the valley stands
Between my own and noble Lara's lands;
My halls from such a guest had honour gain'd,
Nor had Sir Ezzelin his host disdain'd,
But that some previous proof forbade his stay,
And urged him to prepare against to-day;
The word I pledged for his I pledge again,
Or will myself redeem his knighthood's stain.'

He ceased — and Lara answered, 'I am here
To lend at thy demand a listening ear
To tales of evil from a stranger's tongue,
Whose words already might my heart have wrung,

But that I deem'd him scarcely less than mad,
Or, at the worst, a foe ignobly bad.
I know him not — but me it seems he knew
In lands where — but I must not trifle too:
Produce this babbler — or redeem the pledge;
Here in thy hold, and with thy falchion's edge.'

Proud Otho on the instant, reddening, threw
His glove on earth, and forth his sabre flew.
'The last alternative befits me best,
And thus I answer for mine absent guest.'

With cheek unchanging from its sallow gloom,
However near his own or other's tomb;
With hand, whose almost careless coolness spoke
Its grasp well used to deal the sabre-stroke;
With eye, though calm, determin'd not to spare,
Did Lara too his willing weapon bare.
In vain the circling chieftains round them closed,
For Otho's frenzy would not be opposed;
And from his lip those words of insult fell —
His sword is good who can maintain them well.

Short was the conflict; furious, blindly rash,
Vain Otho gave his bosom to the gash:
He bled, and fell; but not with deadly wound,
Stretch'd by a dexterous sleight along the ground.
'Demand thy life!' He answer'd not: and then
From that red floor he ne'er had risen again,
For Lara's brow upon the moment grew
Almost to blackness in its demon hue;
And fiercer shook his angry falchion now
Than when his foe's was levell'd at his brow;
Then all was stern collectedness and art,
Now rose the unleaven'd hatred of his heart;
So little sparing to the foe he fell'd,
That when the approaching crowd his arm withheld,
He almost turn'd the thirsty point on those
Who thus for mercy dared to interpose;
But to a moment's thought that purpose bent;
Yet look'd he on him still with eye intent,
As if he loathed the ineffectual strife
That left a foe, howe'er o'ercome, with life;
As if to search how far the wound he gave
Had sent its victim onward to his grave.

V

They raised the bleeding Otho, and the Leech
Forbade all present question, sign, and speech:
The others met within a neighbouring hall,
And he, incensed, and heedless of them all,
The cause and conqueror in this sudden fray,
In haughty silence slowly strode away;
He back'd his steed, his homeward path he took,
Nor cast on Otho's towers a single look.

VI

But where was he? that meteor of a night,
Who menaced but to disappear with light.
Where was this Ezzelin? who came and went,
To leave no other trace of his intent.
He left the dome of Otho long ere morn,
In darkness, yet so well the path was worn
He could not miss it: near his dwelling lay;
But there he was not, and with coming day
Came fast inquiry, which unfolded nought,
Except the absence of the chief it sought.
A chamber tenantless, a steed at rest,
His host alarm'd, his murmuring squires distress'd:

Their search extends along, around the path,
In dread to meet the marks of prowlers' wrath:
But none are there, and not a brake hath borne
Nor gout of blood, nor shred of mantle torn;
Nor fall nor struggle hath defaced the grass,
Which still retains a mark where murder was;
Nor dabbling fingers left to tell the tale,
The bitter print of each convulsive nail,
When agonised hands that cease to guard,
Wound in the pang that smoothness of the sward.
Some such had been, if here a life was reft,
But these were not; and doubting hope is left;
And strange suspicion, whispering Lara's name,
Now daily mutters o'er his blacken'd fame;
Then sudden silent when his form appear'd,
Awaits the absence of the thing it fear'd,
Again its wonted wondering to renew,
And dye conjecture with a darker hue.

VII

Days roll along, and Otho's wounds are heal'd,
But not his pride; and hate no more conceal'd:
He was a man of power, and Lara's foe,
The friend of all who sought to work him woe,

121

And from his country's justice now demands
Account of Ezzelin at Lara's hands.
Who else than Lara could have cause to fear
His presence? who had made him disappear,
If not the man on whom his menaced charge
Had sate too deeply were he left at large?
The general rumour ignorantly loud,
The mystery dearest to the curious crowd;
The seeming friendlessness of him who strove
To win no confidence, and wake no love;
The sweeping fierceness which his soul betray'd,
The skill with which he wielded his keen blade;
Where had his arm unwarlike caught that art?
Where had that fierceness grown upon his heart?
For it was not the blind capricious rage
A word can kindle and a word assuage;
But the deep working of a soul unmix'd
With aught of pity where its wrath had fix'd;
Such as long power and overgorged success
Concentrates into all that's merciless:
These, link'd with that desire which ever sways
Mankind, the rather to condemn than praise,
'Gainst Lara gathering raised at length a storm,
Such as himself might fear, and foes would form,

And he must answer for the absent head
Of one that haunts him still, alive or dead.

VIII

Within that land was many a malcontent,
Who cursed the tyranny to which he bent;
That soil full many a wringing despot saw
Who work'd his wantonness in form of law;
Long war without and frequent broil within
Had made a path for blood and giant sin,
That waited but a signal to begin
New havoc, such as civil discord blends,
Which knows no neuter, owns but foes or friends;
Fix'd in his feudal fortress each was lord,
In word and deed obey'd, in soul abhorr'd.
Thus Lara had inherited his lands,
And with them pining hearts and sluggish hands;
But that long absence from his native clime
Had left him stainless of oppression's crime,
And how, diverted by his milder sway,
All dread by slow degrees had worn away.
The menials felt their usual awe alone,
But more for him than them that fear was grown;

They deem'd him now unhappy, though at first
Their evil judgment augur'd of the worst,
And each long restless night, and silent mood,
Was traced to sickness, fed by solitude:
And though his lonely habits threw of late
Gloom o'er his chamber, cheerful was his gate;
For thence the wretched ne'er unsoothed withdrew,
For them, at least, his soul compassion knew.
Cold to the great, contemptuous to the high,
The humble pass'd not his unheeding eye;
Much he would speak not, but beneath his roof
They found asylum oft, and ne'er reproof.
And they who watch'd might mark that, day by day,
Some new retainers gather'd to his sway;
But most of late, since Ezzelin was lost,
He play'd the courteous lord and bounteous host:
Perchance his strife with Otho made him dread
Some snare prepared for his obnoxious head;
Whate'er his view, his favour more obtains
With these, the people, than his fellow thanes.
If this were policy, so far 'twas sound,
The million judged but of him as they found;
From him by sterner chiefs to exile driven
They but required a shelter, and 'twas given.

By him no peasant mourn'd his rifled cot,
And scarce the Serf could murmur o'er his lot;
With him old avarice found its hoard secure,
With him contempt forbore to mock the poor;
Youth present cheer and promised recompense
Detain'd, till all too late to part from thence:
To hate he offer'd, with the coming change,
The deep reversion of delay'd revenge;
To love, long baffled by the unequal match,
The well-won charms success was sure to snatch.
All now was ripe, he waits but to proclaim
That slavery nothing which was still a name.
The moment came, the hour when Otho thought
Secure at last the vengeance which he sought:
His summons found the destined criminal
Begirt by thousands in his swarming hall,
Fresh from their feudal fetters newly riven,
Defying earth, and confident of heaven.
That morning he had freed the soil-bound slaves,
Who dig no land for tyrants but their graves!
Such is their cry — some watchword for the fight
Must vindicate the wrong, and warp the right;
Religion — freedom — vengeance — what you will,
A word's enough to raise mankind to kill;

Some factious phrase by cunning caught and spread,
That guilt may reign, and wolves and worms be fed!

Throughout that clime the feudal chiefs had gain'd
Such sway, their infant monarch hardly reign'd;
Now was the hour for faction's rebel growth,
The Serfs contemn'd the one, and hated both:
They waited but a leader, and they found
One to their cause inseparably bound;
By circumstance compell'd to plunge again,
In self-defence, amidst the strife of men.
Cut off by some mysterious fate from those
Whom birth and nature meant not for his foes,
Had Lara from that night, to him accurst,
Prepared to meet, but not alone, the worst:
Some reason urged, whate'er it was, to shun
Inquiry into deeds at distance done;
By mingling with his own the cause of all,
E'en if he fail'd, he still delay'd his fall.
The sullen calm that long his bosom kept,
The storm that once had spent itself and slept,
Roused by events that seem'd foredoom'd to urge
His gloomy fortunes to their utmost verge,

126

Burst forth, and made him all he once had been,
And is again; he only changed the scene.
Light care had he for life, and less for fame,
But not less fitted for the desperate game:
He deem'd himself mark'd out for others' hate,
And mock'd at ruin so they shared his fate.
What cared he for the freedom of the crowd?
He raised the humble but to bend the proud.
He had hoped quiet in his sullen lair,
But man and destiny beset him there:
Inured to hunters, he was found at bay;
And they must kill, they cannot snare the prey.
Stern, unambitious, silent, he had been
Henceforth a calm spectator of life's scene;
But dragg'd again upon the arena, stood
A leader not unequal to the feud;
In voice, mien, gesture, savage nature spoke,
And from his eye the gladiator broke.

X

What boots the oft-repeated tale of strife,
The feast of vultures, and the waste of life?
The varying fortune of each separate field,
The fierce that vanquish, and the faint that yield?

The smoking ruin, and the crumbled wall?
In this the struggle was the same with all;
Save that distempr'd passions lent their force
In bitterness that banish'd all remorse.
None sued, for Mercy knew her cry was vain,
The captive died upon the battle-plain:
In either cause, one rage alone possess'd
The empire of the alternate victor's breast;
And they that smote for freedom or for sway,
Deem'd few were slain, while more remain'd to slay.
It was too late to check the wasting brand,
And Desolation reap'd the famish'd land;
The torch was lighted, and the flame was spread,
And Carnage smiled upon her daily dead.

XI

Fresh with the nerve the new-born impulse strung,
The first success to Lara's numbers clung:
But that vain victory hath ruin'd all;
They form no longer to their leader's call:
In blind confusion on the foe they press,
And think to snatch is to secure success.
The lust of booty, and the thirst of hate,

Lure on the broken brigands to their fate:
In vain he doth whate'er a chief may do,
To check the headlong fury of that crew;
In vain their stubborn ardour he would tame,
The hand that kindles cannot quench the flame;
The wary foe alone hath turn'd their mood,
And shown their rashness to that erring brood:
The feign'd retreat, the nightly ambuscade,
The daily harass, and the fight delay'd,
The long privation of the hoped supply,
The tentless rest beneath the humid sky,
The stubborn wall that mocks the leaguer's art,
And palls the patience of his baffled heart,
Of these they had not deem'd: the battleday
They could encounter as a veteran may;
But more preferr'd the fury of the strife,
And present death, to hourly suffering life:
And famine wrings, and fever sweeps away
His numbers melting fast from their array;
Intemperate triumph fades to discontent,
And Lara's soul alone seems still unbent:
But few remain to aid his voice and hand,
And thousands dwindled to a scanty band:
Desperate, though few, and last and best remain'd

To mourn the discipline they late disdain'd.
One hope survives, the frontier is not far,
And thence they may escape from native war;
And bear within them to the neighbouring state
An exile's sorrows, or an outlaw's hate:
Hard is the task their father-land to quit,
But harder still to perish or submit.

XII

It is resolved — they march — consenting Night
Guides with her star their dim and torchless flight;
Already they perceive its tranquil beam
Sleep on the surface of the barrier stream;
Already they descry — Is yon the bank?
Away! 'tis lined with many a hostile rank.
Return or fly! — What glitters in the rear?
'Tis Otho's banner — the pursuer's spear!
Are those the shepherds' fires upon the height?
Alas! they blaze too widely for the flight:
Cut off from hope, and compass'd in the toil,
Less blood perchance hath bought a richer spoil!

XIII

A moment's pause — 'tis but to breathe their band,
Or shall they onward press, or here withstand?
It matters little — if they charge the foes
Who by their border-stream their march oppose,
Some few, perchance, may break and pass the line,
However link'd to baffle such design.
'The charge be ours! to wait for their assault
Were fate well worthy of a coward's halt.'
Forth flies each sabre, rein'd is every steed,
And the next word shall scarce outstrip the deed:
In the next tone of Lara's gathering breath
How many shall but hear the voice of death!

XIV

His blade is bared — in him there is an air
As deep, but far too tranquil for despair;
A something of indifference more than then
Becomes the bravest, if they feel for men.
He turn'd his eye on Kaled, ever near,
And still too faithful to betray one fear;
Perchance 'twas but the moon's dim twilight threw
Along his aspect an unwonted hue

Of mournful paleness, whose deep tint express'd
The truth, and not the terror of his breast.
This Lara mark'd, and laid his hand on his:
It trembled not in such an hour as this;
His lip was silent, scarcely beat his heart,
His eye alone proclaim'd, 'We will not part!
Thy band may perish, or thy friends may flee,
Farewell to life, but not adieu to thee!'
The word hath pass'd his lips, and onward driven,
Pours the link'd band through ranks asunder riven:
Well has each steed obey'd the armed heel,
And flash the scimitars, and rings the steel;
Outnumber'd, not outbraved, they still oppose
Despair to daring, and a front to foes;
And blood is mingled with the dashing stream,
Which runs all redly till the morning beam.

XV

Commanding, aiding, animating all,
Where foe appear'd to press, or friend to fall,
Cheer Lara's voice, and waves or strikes his steel,
Inspiring hope himself had ceased to feel.
None fled, for well they knew that flight were vain;
But those that waver turn to smite again,

While yet they find the firmest of the foe
Recoil before their leader's look and blow:
Now girt with numbers, now almost alone,
He foils their ranks, or re-unites his own;
Himself he spared not — once they seem'd to fly —
Now was the time, he waved his hand on high,
And shook — Why sudden droops that plumed crest?
The shaft is sped — the arrow's in his breast!
That fatal gesture left the unguarded side,
And Death has stricken down yon arm of pride.
The word of triumph fainted from his tongue;
That hand, so raised, how droopingly it hung!
But yet the sword instinctively retains,
Though from its fellow shrink the falling reins;
These Kaled snatches: dizzy with the blow,
And senseless bending o'er his saddle-bow,
Perceives not Lara that his anxious page
Beguiles his charger from the combat's rage:
Meantime his followers charge, and charge again;
Too mix'd the slayers now to heed the slain!

XVI

Day glimmers on the dying and the dead,
The cloven cuirass and the helmless head;

The war-horse masterless is on the earth,
And that last gasp hath burst his bloody girth;
And near, yet quivering with what life remain'd,
The heel that urged him and the hand that rein'd;
And some too near that rolling torrent lie,
Whose waters mock the lip of those that die;
That panting thirst which scorches in the breath
Of those that die the soldier's fiery death,
In vain impels the burning mouth to crave
One drop — the last — to cool it for the grave;
With feeble and convulsive effort swept,
Their limbs along the crimson'd turf have crept;
The faint remains of life such struggles waste,
But yet they reach the stream and bend to taste:
They feel its freshness, and almost partake —
Why pause? No further thirst have they to slake —
It is unquench'd, and yet they feel it not;
It was an agony — but now forgot!

XVII

Beneath a lime, remoter from the scene,
Where but for him that strife had never been,
A breathing but devoted warrior lay:
'Twas Lara bleeding fast from life away.

His follower once, and now his only guide,
Kneels Kaled watchful o'er his welling side,
And with his scarf would stanch the tides that rush,
With each convulsion, in a blacker gush;
And then, as his faint breathing waxes low,
In feebler, not less fatal tricklings flow:
He scarce can speak, but motions him 'tis vain,
And merely adds another throb to pain.
He clasps the hand that pang which would assuage,
And sadly smiles his thanks to that dark page,
Who nothing fears, nor feels, nor heeds, nor sees,
Save that damp brow which rests upon his knees;
Save that pale aspect, where the eye, though dim,
Held all the light that shone on earth for him.

XVIII

The foe arrives, who long had search'd the field,
Their triumph nought till Lara too should yield:
They would remove him, but they see 'twere vain,
And he regards them with a calm disdain,
That rose to reconcile him with his fate,
And that escape to death from living hate;
And Otho comes, and leaping from his steed,
Looks on the bleeding foe that made him bleed,

And questions of his state; he answers not,
Scarce glances on him as on one forgot;
And turns to Kaled: — each remaining word
They understood not, if distinctly heard;
His dying tones are in that other tongue,
To which some strange remembrance wildly clung.
They spake of other scenes, but what — is known
To Kaled, whom their meaning reach'd alone;
And he replied, though faintly, to their sound,
While gazed the rest in dumb amazement round:
They seem'd even then — that twain — unto the last
To half-forget the present in the past;
To share between themselves some separate fate,
Whose darkness none beside should penetrate.

XIX

Their words though faint were many — from the tone
Their import those who heard could judge alone;
From this, you might have deem'd young Kaled's death
More near than Lara's by his voice and breath,
So sad, so deep, and hesitating broke
The accents his scarce-moving pale lips spoke;
But Lara's voice, though low, at first was clear
And calm, till murmuring death gasp'd hoarsely near;

But from his visage little could we guess,
So unrepentant, dark, and passionless,
Save that when struggling nearer to his last,
Upon that page his eye was kindly cast;
And once, as Kaled's answering accents ceased,
Rose Lara's hand, and pointed to the East:
Whether (as then the breaking sun from high
Roll'd back the clouds) the morrow caught his eye,
Or that 'twas chance, or some remember'd scene,'
That raised his arm to point where such had been,
Scarce Kaled seem'd to know, but turn'd away,
As if his heart abhorr'd that coming day,
And shrunk his glance before that morning light,
To look on Lara's brow — where all grew night.
Yet sense seem'd left, though better were its loss;
For when one near display'd the absolving cross,
And proffer'd to his touch the holy bead,
Of which his parting soul might own the need,
He look'd upon it with an eye profane,
And smiled — Heaven pardon! if 'twere with disdain:
And Kaled, though he spoke not, nor withdrew
From Lara's face his fix'd despairing view,
With brow repulsive, and with gesture swift,
Flung back the hand which held the sacred gift,

As if such but disturb'd the expiring man,
Nor seem'd to know his life but then began,
That life of Immortality, secure
To none, save them whose faith in Christ is sure.

XX

But gasping heaved the breath that Lara drew,
And dull the film along his dim eye grew;
His limbs stretch'd fluttering, and his head droop'd o'er
The weak yet still untiring knee that bore;
He press'd the hand he held upon his heart —
It beats no more, but Kaled will not part
With the cold grasp, but feels, and feels in vain,
For that faint throb which answers not again.
'It beats!' — Away, thou dreamer! he is gone —
It once was Lara which thou look'st upon.

XXI

He gazed, as if not yet has pass'd away
The haughty spirit of that humbled clay;
And those around have roused him from his trance,
But cannot tear from thence his fixed glance;
And when, in raising him from where he bore
Within his arms the form that felt no more,

He saw the head his breast would still sustain,
Roll down like earth to earth upon the plain;
He did not dash himself thereby, nor tear
The glossy tendrils of his raven hair,
But strove to stand and gaze, but reel'd and fell,
Scarce breathing more than that he loved so well.
Than that he loved! Oh! never yet beneath
The breast of man such trusty love may breathe!
That trying moment hath at once reveal'd
The secret long and yet but half conceal'd;
In baring to revive that lifeless breast,
Its grief seem'd ended, but the sex confess'd;
And life return'd, and Kaled felt no shame —
What now to her was Womanhood or Fame?

XXII

And Lara sleeps not where his fathers sleep,
But where he died his grave was dug as deep;
Nor is his mortal slumber less profound,
Though priest nor bless'd nor marble deck'd the mound,
And he was mourn'd by one whose quiet grief,
Less loud, outlasts a people's for their chief.
Vain was all question ask'd her of the past,
And vain e'en menace — silent to the last;

She told nor whence, nor why she left behind
Her all for one who seem'd but little kind.
Why did she love him? Curious fool! — be still —
Is human love the growth of human will?
To her he might be gentleness; the stern
Have deeper thoughts than your dull eyes discern,
And when they love, your smilers guess not how
Beats the strong heart, though less the lips avow.
They were not common links, that form'd the chain
That bound to Lara Kaled's heart and brain;
But that wild tale she brook'd not to unfold,
And seal'd is now each lip that could have told.

XXIII

They laid him in the earth, and on his breast,
Besides the wound that sent his soul to rest,
They found the scatter'd dints of many a scar,
Which were not planted there in recent war;
Where'er had pass'd his summer years of life,
It seems they vanish'd in a land of strife;
But all unknown his glory or his guilt,
These only told that somewhere blood was spilt,
And Ezzelin, who might have spoke the past,
Return'd no more — that night appear'd his last.

Upon that night (a peasant's is the tale)
A Serf that cross'd the intervening vale,
When Cynthia's light almost gave way to morn,
And nearly veil'd in mist her waning horn;
A Serf, that rose betimes to thread the wood,
And hew the bough that brought his children's food,
Pass'd by the river that divides the plain
Of Otho's lands and Lara's broad domain:
He heard a tramp — a horse and horseman broke
From out the wood — before him was a cloak
Wrapt round some burthen at his saddlebow,
Bent was his head, and hidden was his brow.
Roused by the sudden sight at such a time,
And some foreboding that it might be crime.
Himself unheeded watch'd the stranger's course,
Who reach'd the river, bounded from his horse,
And lifting thence the burthen which he bore,
Heaved up the bank, and dash'd it from the shore,
Then paused, and look'd, and turn'd, and seem'd to watch,
And still another hurried glance would snatch,
And follow with his step the stream that flow'd,
As if even yet too much its surface show'd;

At once he started, stoop'd, around him strown
The winter floods had scatter'd heaps of stone;
Of these the heaviest thence he gather'd there,
And slung them with a more than common care.
Meantime the Serf had crept to where unseen
Himself might safely mark what this might mean;
He caught a glimpse, as of a floating breast,
And something glitter'd starlike on the vest;
But ere he well could mark the buoyant trunk,
A massy fragment smote it, and it sunk:
It rose again, but indistinct to view,
And left the waters of a purple hue,
Then deeply disappear'd: the horseman gazed
Till ebb'd the latest eddy it had raised;
Then turning, vaulted on his pawing steed,
And instant spurr'd him into panting speed.
His face was mask'd — the features of the dead,
If dead it were, escaped the observer's dread;
But if in sooth a star its bosom bore,
Such is the badge that knighthood ever wore,
And such 'tis known Sir Ezzelin had worn
Upon the night that led to such a morn.
If thus he perish'd, Heaven receive his soul!
His undiscover'd limbs to ocean roll;

And charity upon the hope would dwell
It was not Lara's hand by which he fell.

XXV

And Kaled — Lara — Ezzelin, are gone,
Alike without their monumental stone!
The first, all efforts vainly strove to wean
From lingering where her chieftain's blood had been:
Grief had so tamed a spirit once to proud,
Her tears were few, her wailing never loud;
But furious would you tear her from the spot
Where yet she scarce believed that he was not,
Her eye shot forth with all the living fire
That haunts the tigress in her whelpless ire;
But left to waste her wary moments there,
She talk'd all idly unto shapes of air,
Such as the busy brain of Sorrow paints,
And woos to listen to her fond complaints:
And she would sit beneath the very tree
Where lay his drooping head upon her knee:
And in that posture where she saw him fall,
His words, his looks, his dying grasp recall;
And she had shorn, but saved her raven hair,
And oft would snatch it from her bosom there,

And fold, and press it gently to the ground,
As if she staunch'd anew some phantom's wound.
Herself would question, and for him reply;
Then rising, start, and beckon him to fly
From some imagined spectre in pursuit;
Then seat her down upon some linden's root,
And hide her visage with her meagre hand,
Or trace strange characters along the sand.
This could not last — she lies by him she loved;
Her tale untold, her truth too dearly proved.